*10 Easy Steps To...*

# Finding
# Your Ideal
# SOULMATE!

*10 Easy Steps To...*

# Finding
# Your Ideal
# SOULMATE!

*Elaine Sihera*

AnSer
publishing

First published in Great Britain 2006 by AnSer Publishing.

AnSer Publishing
Maidenhead
Berkshire
Email: easysteps@elainesihera.co.uk

© *Elaine Sihera* 2006

**British Library Cataloguing in Publication Data**.

A CIP record of this book is available on request from the British Library.

ISBN 0 9517341 4 8

*Printed and bounded in Great Britain by:*
Evonprint Ltd
Small Dole
West Sussex

*To Terry Price and his wife, Pauline.*
*With more thanks than I can ever express*
*for their contribution to my journey.*

✳ ✳ ✳ ✳ ✳

*Love is not automatic. It takes conscious*
*practice and awareness, just like playing the*
*piano or golf. However, you have ample*
*opportunities to practise.*
*Everyone you meet can be your practice session.*

Doc Childre and Sara Paddison

**Special thanks to Alex Wing** without whose contribution to creating this series, and ensuring it was registered, this book might not have seen the light of day.

## Other books by the Author

### *Personal and Career*

○ Money, Sex & Compromise (£14.95)

○ What's In A Name?

○ Signposts To Success

### *Human Resource Management*

○ Managing the Diversity Maze (£89.95)

○ Heads Under Pressure

❋ ❋ ❋ ❋ ❋ ❋

*Each of us at any time and space is doing the
very best we can with what we have.*

Louise L. Hay

# ~ The Author ~

Known as "Miss Diversity", because of her background and expertise, Elaine Sihera is a leading African Caribbean writer, editor and publisher in the U.K. Born in Jamaica, Elaine emigrated to the UK in 1967. She read English and Social Sciences at the Open University (its first African Caribbean graduate) then completed her post-graduate at Cambridge University.

Author of *Managing the Diversity Maze*, an appraisal of the concept, history and application of diversity in human resource management, Elaine is the leading independent authority on diversity issues in Europe. Anti-ageist, pro-feminist and anti-racist, this former education manager is not only a tireless campaigner for fairness and justice, but also a leading speaker on social issues in Britain, having founded, respectively, the very successful annual British Diversity Awards and Windrush Men and Women Achiever of the Year Awards.

A confident, people-oriented achiever, whose watchword is RESPECT, Elaine has also turned her attention to personal advice and empowerment and this is her second book in the field. *Money, Sex and Compromise*, on the hidden agenda within relationships and why they fail, was her first contribution.

More articles, self-assessment quizzes, personal guidance and information on improving relationships, and life, are available on **www.elainesihera.co.uk**.

# ~ Acknowledgements ~

This book is dedicated to lovers and couples everywhere, especially those in long relationships who have unselfishly devoted their lives to one another. I too have been blessed in my life and loves and would like to give sincere credit to, and celebrate, some very special people who have made it possible for me to find my own happiness and purpose.

Great thanks and gratitude to Lord Michael Chan and his lovely wife, Lady Irene, whose contribution to my work has been unquestioning and special. Thanks also to Aston Johnson, who has been there like a rock, in my good times and bad, hoping that this book shortens his search and helps him to find his true soulmate.

Loving thanks also to my sisters Marjorie Griffiths-Clark in Jamaica and Belmora Maitland (Joyce) in Canada, whose continuing motivation has inspired me to write this book in record time, and to a truly warm person, Peter C.R who came into my life at just the right moment to make that difference. I hope he too finds some inspiration for his ideal mate.

Grateful thanks to Geri Poulton, Barbara Perry, Ayesha Azam, Marigold Nunes and Bubbles White for their wonderful friendship and encouragement at this key point in my life. I hope this work will inspire them to discover their true greatness and their own loving soulmates.

To golden couples, Neslyn and Peter Watson Druée and Tom and Heather Brown. Hope you continue with your mutual and caring support of one another. Also for Martin Rowland and Jackie, whose loyal understanding of, and faith in, me have been unwavering. Sometimes life does not work out as we hope, but there is *always* a silver lining. I send heartfelt thanks for all your tremendous help and support.

Sincere gratitude to Mike Peters for the blind faith and trust in me. Thanks for taking me forward to a new level of discovery. I hope you too find the person of your dreams. To Marco Santos, for flashing that warm, dazzling smile of encouragement to continually remind me of what I had to do to finish this book, and to the great Richard 'O', hoping this helps him to identify and work on the gaps in his marriage.

To a great business manager, Michelle Hogg. Thank you for being there and believing in the dream in the face of all the odds. It is most appreciated. I hope you too find some inspiration here.

Last but not least, to my super editor, Terry Cattermole, whose unstinting efforts greatly improved the narrative and reduced the ambiguities. I really cannot thank you enough.

# ~ CONTENTS ~

# ~ INTRODUCTION ~

## <u>The Love of My Life</u>

**I** have fallen deeply in love three times during my life so far and they were all intense affairs that ended with unresolved feelings. The first time was with my ex-husband. It lasted 33 years and was a roller-coaster of incredible proportions, marked by some great loving, caring and appreciation at the beginning, and resentment, anger and frustration at the end. When we finally parted, there was still a lot of attraction but much sadness between us.

Halfway through my marriage, during a particularly rocky time of womanising by my partner, especially with my best friend, I took refuge with my sister abroad and fell instantly in love with someone I didn't even want to meet. George was incredible in his adoration of me and, though I too was deeply attracted, I was not yet mature enough to deal with this sudden onslaught of new emotions.

My Catholic upbringing also ensured that a stamp of disapproval would have been put on anything that might have developed and I retreated in some confusion. I had no intention of leaving my marriage and the U.K, and thus ignored my feelings – with some difficulty, despite George being steadfast in his pursuit of me. He even flew unexpectedly all the way from Canada to prise me away with a proposal in the classroom where I was teaching! Having seen his perceived ideal, he was not going to relinquish her that easily.

Though he was very resourceful and caring, I don't think I was looking for another partner at that time. I didn't know it then, but I was suffering from the classic form of rejection. I welcomed affirmation and attention, but got much more than I bargained for! From Canada he pursued me for a few years until he realised I was not going to budge.

Twenty-five years later, when I was single again, this fascinating man would, once more, unexpectedly declare his love for me. But I do not believe in going backwards in time and, as

*10 Easy Steps To....*

flattered as I was, I had already learnt the lesson he taught me, so I left well alone, opting for his friendship instead.

And then there was David.

## Unfinished Business

I knew him for only two years of my life, after leaving my marriage, and fought off his attentions for three months before agreeing to meet him, but he has had the most profound effect on me since, much more than I can ever comprehend. I suppose we have some unfinished business because when we 'parted' it was in the most loving way possible. The moment was not an ideal one for us to fall in love because of our circumstances, but one can never dictate what will happen next in one's life. So I accept it with grace and gratitude because he came into my life at precisely the right moment.

For me, David is the love of my life. He inspired my first book on relationships (*Money, Sex and Compromise*), but, even more so, he has inspired this important one too. If I were to score him using the 10 steps in this book, he would get at least eight, as well as scoring 90 per cent for satisfying my top five values! No one else I have met has come even close to that. In fact, we liked doing quizzes and always scored very highly with regard to one another, even when we completed them separately. I recall writing in my diary one day that, 'David is 10 per cent short of heaven'! I was incredibly happy during our friendship, just wanting to smile all the time, feeling alive and fulfilled. In short, he came close to what I regard as MY ideal soulmate, and might well, unconsciously, act as a litmus test for any others to come.

Tall, slim, distinguished and good-looking, resilient, brainy and very successful, David was in a class of his own because he knew who he was and revelled in being himself (Step One). Professionally, he knew what he wanted and where he wanted to go (Step Two) and worked steadfastly towards attaining it. He also knew what he stood for and could defend it with a passion (Step Three), but was happy enough in his own skin to allow me to be what I wanted too without feeling threatened.

I remember the discussions we had regarding

the Iraq War (he was for, I was against). I had a counterpoint for every point he made and he often found it frustrating when he failed to affect my views on the possible outcomes. However, at the end of each 'debate', after agreeing to differ, he would hug me, look deeply into my eyes, tell me how 'beautiful and intelligent' I was, and that he just wanted to love me. It was an amazing relationship of reciprocity, mutual reinforcement and mutual affirmation.

## Two Magnets

Best of all, David fulfilled the three main areas of attraction almost 100 per cent (Step Four). The physical chemistry between us was often so overpowering, we just wanted to touch and hold each other all the time. As he said, we were like 'two magnets', unable to keep themselves apart from one another; feelings that generated great passion and excitement between us. The emotional bonding being unusually deep, it fuelled an intense desire to communicate (Step Five) and connect with each other at every possible moment. We spent hours on the telephone each day. Even when I went to visit my sisters in Jamaica for four weeks, the calls continued almost daily. By the last week of my holiday, he was missing me so much, the length of the calls had stretched to over an hour every day!

The intellectual fit between us was outstanding too – an engineer with his logical and analytical approach, firmly rooted in inanimate form and structure, matched easily with the social fixer, her love of people and adept skills in social interaction. We complemented each other superbly in many other ways.

He liked to challenge my views on fate, destiny and spirituality in order to gain a greater understanding of them, and to convince himself of their worth, while I also challenged his seemingly cold, mechanical and pragmatic view of the world. Considering that we were both in our mid-50s, and virtually 'chalk and cheese', this was some incredible, unexpected love affair across cultures, across race and across perspectives.

We behaved like teenagers, enveloped in the sheer joy and passion of such a satisfying rela-

18

tionship – a kind only dreamt of at this late stage of our lives.


## Fantastic Warmth

We had few expectations of each other (Step Six), allowing for individual growth and the unfolding of our characters without seeking to change anything in each other. We accepted our faults and foibles as part of the overall attraction. They were key parts of our personalities which made us the unique people we were. We also liked the flexibility to appreciate the imperfect within us.

David was the most skilled listener I had come across (Step Five), and seemed to truly revel in his curiosity. He never forgot anything he heard and was always back with a follow-up question. He took great pride, and a keen interest, in my work and my aspirations, always wanting to know the details of my day, or the state of my latest project. Nothing was too good to do for me or to give me. He also liked to suggest an alternative solution to any dilemma, especially if he felt I needed one.

We respected and trusted each other greatly (Step Nine) and often discussed former partners and what they had taught us. There was also his wonderfully dead-pan sense of humour (Step Four), his devilish chuckle and mesmerising green eyes – but that's another story! I felt truly wanted, appreciated and loved.

Most noticeable of all, the relationship between David and myself was marked by total reciprocity (Step Seven) – mutual giving and affirmation. I learned the true meaning of that word through our love and it was quite an experience for me to give and receive in equal measure. I felt total excitement when dealing with him. His encouragement was so inspiring. He wanted everything I had to give and returned it in abundance to me and the experience was awesome.

We did not live together and I remember an occasion when he was visiting me after work, travelling on the motorway from Bristol (where he lived) and a lorry overturned halting his journey. He was only 12 miles out of the city, but he refused to turn back. Three hours later than planned, he pulled up outside my door. He came inside, stopped for a moment, looked at me lovingly, and with a great smile of achievement on his face, said: "While I was stuck on the motorway, I did wonder why I was putting myself out at this time of the evening to see you, after a long, hard day at work. Then I arrive here and look at you and I know why."

Since we both liked our own time and space, it was magical when we met. Being with him was so passionate and exquisite. Often we would just sit or lie together and stare at each other for ages in a kind of wonder at what was happening between us, unable to fathom the intensity of the attraction.

But that is the truth about love and reciprocity – we feel fantastic because of it and will go to the ends of the earth for those we love. Nothing is too difficult to do for them. When we don't want to oblige, this means that crucial Step Seven is missing, which then signals a rocky road of resentment and disappointment ahead.

\* \* \* \* \* \*

*Everything that irritates us about others can lead us to an understanding of ourselves.*

Carl Jung

## Key Inspiration

I have made much of David's positive points, which might imply that he was perfect or that I wore rose-tinted lenses. However, we were firmly rooted in reality. Indeed, he had quite a few irritating faults, and so did I. For example, he could be intransigent when he wanted to be, and I could be equally stubborn. We just didn't dwell on these faults. We might comment on them jokingly, but we preferred to celebrate our strengths because the relationship was so powerful.

That is also the point of connecting together – namely, mutual celebration, not to put each other down or focus upon our weaknesses. He was satisfied with the way he was and did not wish to be any different, and I was satisfied with me too. But this was not always the case.

When I first met him he was an unhappy individual who suddenly came upon a type of love he had never had before and which astounded, excited and frightened him in equal measure. He always said that he did not deserve such love and affection and that I was too besotted with him, but he was secretly thrilled with it and responded in kind.

He lived a comfortable, affluent life, after having fought his way from setbacks. For this reason he was full of fears about his future, too afraid to take any life-changing decisions that might alter his material balance in any way, especially at his age. This meant that while I felt energised by such a warm, generous and encouraging individual, believing that with the right person beside me I could move mountains, his past negative experiences and personal fears blinded him to what was possible. This led to opposite views on our future. It took me a while, but I learnt to appreciate the difference in our perspectives, though I respected him for it.

He will always love me, he kept saying, and the fact that he is the key inspiration for two of my books speaks volumes for his effect upon me. We were besotted with one another, yet couldn't explain it. So I have spent the months apart from him working out the ingredients of such an amazing love match, identifying what really lay behind it, and have come up with these 10 steps.

## Separate Ways

We are no longer an item, not because our love has diminished in any way, but because we needed to move such deep feelings on to another level. We couldn't agree on the new direction and agreed to differ. It was a most difficult time for us. He described it as 'very traumatic' being away from me in the first few months. Our love was so strong that, while the average romance is heady in the first six months or year, then cools to something more realistic and routine, ours just kept growing, getting better and better, never leaving the 'honeymoon' stage at all, even after two years of seeing each other!

I laughed until I cried one day when I read that the 'average' couple in the U.K. made love about four times per month. We were doing more than that per week, having the most amazingly passionate lovemaking, with only distance and time preventing us from indulging more often!

Will he come back into my life? Perhaps not. Some people are just guides to our purpose and the baton has to be passed on. It would be a shame to permanently lose what we had, especially as we still have some issues to resolve. Moreover, we would make a fabulous professional team because his skills would certainly complement mine. But, as we are constantly evolving, any reunion depends on where we both are in our lives at that point in time. By then, we are likely to be two different people needing different things for our fulfilment, and might even have met other ideal soulmates.

So, I am moving on with my life with the hope that someone even better (if that's possible!) will be sharing the rich love and emotion I have to give. For me, the huge difference between the pre-David and post-David era is that, before I met him, I was feeling negative, low and confused about who I was and where I was going. I felt like a victim – loveless and unsure of what love itself really meant.

After my time with him I now know who I am, where I am heading, what I want from life and, above all, what I want from love and a relationship – a very powerful change that makes him a hard act to follow!

## Reasons for Soulmates

Whenever we search for a partner we tend to expect that only someone permanent is likely to come into our life, so we keep looking for the 'perfect' one to share it. But it is my belief that soulmates come into our lives for four main reasons, three of which are temporary in nature and only one permanent. They arrive to:

A. *Teach us something significant, and or-*

B. *Lead us out of a stressful time or crisis situation, and or-*

C. *Enhance our feelings of self-worth and boost our wellbeing for the next stage in our life, and or-*

D. *Be the BIG ONE – the ideal and permanent soulmate we seek.*

Most hurt within relationships arises from having the wrong expectations of partners because we like to see every date as leading to potential permanence (Reason D). We burden each new friendship with our need for long-term security only to find that it was not as permanent as we had hoped. We then overlook the message we were given by belittling or negating the experience. But any relationship always prepares us for dealing more competently with the next one. It's our ego, failed expectations and acute disappointment which prevent us from appreciating what we learned while encouraging us to vilify our partners instead.

Feeling hurt, we fail to learn the message because of our need for scapegoats. We then continue to repeat the pain with every subsequent partner until we change our pattern of reaction. The best approach is to allow our relationships to unfold, without too much analysis or too many expectations, while being prepared for any outcome. You are likely to be very surprised while learning a lot. For example, while my ex-husband was my ideal soulmate for over three decades, David was in my life to teach me something new and to lead me out of a crisis. I knew we wouldn't be permanent, even though I hoped we would be. He was in transition himself. I also did not wish to settle down with someone so soon after my long marriage.

I have thus learned that lesson of love and am now passing it on. Though I have missed him, I can appreciate what we had without any rancour because I benefited from having him in my life and understood why it was not to last longer. He has no animosity toward me either, always affirming me in every way, and commenting on what a 'remarkable person' I am. I assume that he greatly appreciated my presence too and gained significantly from it.

## Reason for Closeness

If I could single out just one reason for our close-ness I would say it was our values. We shared almost the same values in our perspectives but with enough differences to make the relation-ship interesting and to keep it fresh. We both love discussions as well as periods of solitude. We both believed in respect for the individual and in making a difference to our world in some form by supporting and empowering others. We were also very confident individuals who appre-ciated each other without feeling any form of jealousy or competition. We celebrated one another as special people and never failed to affirm each other daily. Above all, we were both very loving individuals who just wanted to share that love with each other as much as possible.

Sadly, many couples have compromised their values to such an extent that they are not even sure of what they want or stand for anymore and, as a result, are perpetually unhappy. But when we forego our core desires or go against our cherished beliefs, we can never feel good about ourselves.

For example, one abiding image I took away from my marriage was the television being on each and every evening and of having to speak over it when I wanted to talk with my partner. He grew fearful of every conversation we had turning into a row and kept the television going in the hope that any chat would be brief, while I grew more frustrated at not really being heard. With David, the television was never on unless there was something specific that either one, or both of us, wanted to watch. This meant we had far more time to focus upon, and to connect with, each other.

The difference was stark and enlightening. Such moments gradually revealed to me that, in the latter years of my marriage, I was putting up with many things that went against my core values in the hope that the situation would get better, and I am sure that my partner was doing the same for 'a quiet life'. Sadly, it never did improve until I re-asserted what felt right for me and acted upon it.

## Purpose of This Book

*10 Easy Steps To....Finding Your Ideal Soulmate!* is meant for people (perhaps over 24 years old) who are seriously looking to settle down with someone or desiring a significant partnership; for people in the first phase of their new courtship, who have had only a few dates, or for those who haven't even met their next date yet! These 10 steps should help them be more prepared. However, people already in relationships can also use this book in order to find out which of the 10 steps is missing or why their relationship is failing. Like a checklist, it will reveal the gaps and the blockages. But that's the easy part. The harder bit will be taking the necessary actions to remedy them.

That's where many people fall down because they hope that any problem will either fix itself or that their soulmates will somehow change themselves enough to remedy the situation. But that's just pie in the sky. Change comes from within us, through our thoughts and actions. If we do not change, the situation will simply stay the same, in effect being a rut, or gradually get worse.

If you have been seeking your ideal soulmate without much luck, dive in and see what could be here to inform, motivate and assist you in your search. It could be that your values need aligning with your aspirations. You are probably not clear about what they are and so your love radar is unable to be selective, or to home in on the right person. For example, why date a smoker and then nag her/him to give it up because you don't like smoking? Surely, you shouldn't be courting a smoker in the first place? Such a situation is not really fair to either of you.

❋ ❋ ❋ ❋ ❋ ❋

*The voyage of discovery is not in seeking new landscapes but in having new eyes.*

Marcel Proust

## Making Relationships Work

It is not easy attracting the right person and keeping them for a lifetime, but the fact that I have had little difficulty attracting and keeping some very special men in my life suggests that I must be doing something right. Furthermore, talking with lots of people who have had problems in their relationships, and who have been hurt and frustrated with their outcomes, has also supplied some insights into what is going wrong between couples. I share these unscientific findings with you too.

Of course, *10 Easy Steps To....Finding Your Ideal Soulmate!* is designed to provide only some key insights and answers, not to act as an in-depth exploration of the subject. That is why it is pocket-size! Nevertheless, it does provide that crucial foundation to understanding the issue and knowing how to make your relationships work better.  As such, it is a deliberate taster rather than the full meal. Hopefully, it should lead you to explore other books in the field.

I have also used a simple 10 point rating system throughout the book (the key is in Step

One) to assess your current personal state. Numbers always give a clearer picture than guesswork. They build a distinct structure and also allow for better comparisons. However, they are meaningless in themselves unless they are taken in context and approached with some genuine honesty. Do disclose openly for best results.

Please note too that all the names used in this book to illustrate examples are substitutes for the real ones to protect the people mentioned.


So which of the 10 steps are likely to be missing in your new, or current, relationship? And having discovered it, what are YOU going to do about it from TODAY? That's the most crucial question for you as you begin this short journey of enlightenment.

I also hope that everyone who reads *10 Easy Steps To....Finding Your Ideal Soulmate!* will find their desired companions soon afterwards. And if they are rewarded with even half of what David and I shared in our love, they will be extremely happy and fortunate!

As for me, I would just like to say one thing now: Cheers David! You were there when I needed you most and I will never forget it. Heartfelt thanks for being in my life and for teaching me so much in such a short time, through your unselfish love, encouragement and affirmation. I hope you are having the time of your life too. I send you continued love and best wishes in achieving your dreams!

One small favour to ask of you, dear reader. If you do find someone with the help of this book, let me know by emailing me at
**mystory@elainesihera.com**.
It will be thrilling to hear your good news and it can also be posted on our website, if all is agreeable. Thank you for your interest in my journey and I hope you find it at least informative.

*Elaine Sihera*

✳ ✳ ✳ ✳ ✳ ✳

*Security is mostly a superstition. It does not exist in nature.... Avoiding danger is no safer in the long run than outright exposure.*
*Life is either a daring adventure, or nothing.*

Helen Keller

# ~ STEP ONE ~

## Know Who You Are & Be Yourself

Most of us fear being alone indefinitely. If you are single, or in a bad relationship, what will be your dearest wish today? Could it be to meet someone wonderful to love and cherish you in a kind of mutual appreciation society? Someone to increase your own level of happiness? In short, someone with whom you share very strong chemistry and love?

That's a natural wish, but how do you go about finding this ideal person in the face of so many hit-and-miss attempts and crashing relationships? Speaking from experience, it can be very difficult when you don't know how. There are about 150,000[1] divorces in the U.K each year, which represents just under 40 per cent of marriages.

Put in simple terms, during the one hour it takes you to enjoy your tasty sandwich or gourmet lunch today, 17 families in the U.K will have gone their separate ways. In fact, assuming that you read at a steady pace, by the time you have finished this book, at least 250 more British families will have dissolved their union. Add the break-ups among those who are just living together and you have the true picture. When the figures are put in such stark terms, it is easy to see that too many relationships are simply not working.

In light of these depressing divorce statistics, I might appear to be stating the obvious by telling you that seeking a soulmate for life, or even for six months, is a very important decision. But it is a fact in need of restating. The simple truth is that it gets forgotten as soon as our eyes meet those of the perceived 'chosen one'. Instead, we abandon common sense (or, conversely, we are ruled too much by it) as our familiar patterned behaviour is triggered in the hope of achieving our desires.

The result is that nothing much changes. We go on seeking our soulmate in just the same way we have always done it, which leaves us feeling as disappointed with our life as ever. Hopefully, *10 Easy Steps To....Finding Your Ideal Soulmate!* should remind you of this crucial point as you read the steps and consider their value to your own life.

Each person seeking a soulmate, or stuck in a negative relationship, has a chance of securing a positive outcome for themselves at least 95 per cent of the time and finding the proverbial 'happy ever after' bliss they seek, instead of just accepting what happens to them. This is because you create your own reality so you have much more power than you think. Success in life is 90 percent preparation and only about 10 per cent luck. It has very little to do with whom you might randomly meet but everything to do with YOU, because your unique pattern of reaction is the biggest obstacle to positive results.

## Our Pattern of Reaction

Formed by your childhood and past experiences, this pattern of reaction (essentially your attitude to others and expectations of them) constantly changes and rearranges itself in response to the hurt or happiness you encounter in every step you take. This interactive pattern waits patiently to work its magic, or misery, on some unsuspecting person so that the minute he/she draws your attention, the pattern swings into action.

If it is a positive pattern based primarily upon warm experiences, you won't need this book too much because your life will, no doubt, be 'coming up roses'. You fly in the face of predictions and you are loved, desired and wanted most of the time – congratulations! However, if your pattern of life is like that of most people – one of broken hearts and short-term liaisons, of doubt, insecurity, unhappiness, intermittent loneliness or 'victimhood' – then, once triggered, your pattern of reaction will continue to have negative outcomes.

"If you keep doing what you've always done, you will only keep getting what you've always got," said a wise person some time ago, which explains why your relationships, so far, perhaps have a feeling of déja vu and you might feel as if you are never moving forward. You cannot change the people you meet so you have to start the changes in you.

If you are not getting to the places you wish to go, or you are not enjoying the kind of relationship you should have, future success in your love life now depends on breaking that subtle pattern of reaction for something much more rewarding and exciting! But, first, you have some important work to do.

## Personal Preparation

The key question, as you pick up *10 Easy Steps To....Finding Your Ideal Soulmate!* and curiously wonder whether it could be of any value to you, is this: How prepared are YOU for the next potential soulmate you are likely to meet in your life? For the special person who might be browsing another book in the next aisle? For the one you might bump into as you make your way briskly round the supermarket? For the one who might catch your eye across the pub? Notice that the question relates to you, in particular.

Often we spend so much time focusing on others, trying to change them to suit us, or being unduly wary of them, we deliberately miss key things about ourselves that affect our outcomes. Net result: the other person might change a little, if we are lucky, but we are still reacting with the same inflexible pattern and wondering why we are getting nowhere. If you are not yet prepared but would like to be, that's where this little book comes in to help you avoid repeating your established interactive pattern and to get the usual results. In fact, the suggestions outlined in *10 Easy Steps To....Finding Your Ideal Soulmate!* are like the air you breathe and the water you drink on the next stage of your journey.

The fact that our reaction pattern is often more negative than positive is one reason why, all too often, we end up with something we don't want. Too many people simply find fault with possible dates, or advertise loudly what they do NOT want in a soulmate ("If you're a gold digger, pass me by" or "If you're not 6'2, no way, midget"), wait expectantly and then wonder why they end up with exactly what they feared in the first place!

The reason for this cycle of depressing famili-arity is that we only get what we focus upon. Every thought is a vibration that attracts similar vibrations to it and bring them back to us, fulfilling our desires in the process. However, usually, the only focus or energy we place upon ourself is likely to be negative. As a result, only negative results return to haunt us. If we also don't know who we are or what we want, how do we know what is blocking our progress toward having it? How do we know where we are heading? And, most important, how do we know what really makes us happy?

**Stop here** and use the key below (which should be used wherever a rating is required), to rate your state of general happiness out of 10. By that I mean how you *usually* feel day to day – then rate your feelings so far today.

**9-10** = Excellent;     **3-4.5** = Very Low;
**7-8.5** = Very Good;     **0-2.5** = Non-Existent.
**5-6.5** = Could Be Better;

## Discovering Happiness

You should have two ratings similar to mine: 9 for general and 10 for today (9G/10T) because I am excited about starting this new book. The main point is that there is not much of a gap between my two figures. By comparing the two ratings, you will know when you are really at sea in your emotions. You will then need to work out the reason (or reasons) for any significant discrepancy and address it in some way. For example, mine would be 10 for most of the time if it weren't for one nagging problem in my family life. Once that is sorted, as I know it will be at some point, my general rating should even be 10!

Notice too that the missing factor is worth only one point to me, even though it is extremely important, because if we have to wait for ideal circumstances to be truly happy, we will miss the enjoyment of most of our life. Your daily rating can sink as low as zero, which is quite fine if life is giving you a bum deal that day. However, if your general score is 4.5 or under, you have some chronic issues or fears to sort out, otherwise that is how you will feel all of the time, regardless of the good things that may happen to you. That is a sad way to live each day.

Low happiness levels actually prevent you from appreciating the great blessings and people in your life and encourage you to take them for granted. Your feelings dictate how you perceive the world and how others treat you in turn. The two go hand-in-hand, acting upon each other in a demotivating circle.

That explains why some people seem to be constantly miserable and pessimistic whereas some are the complete opposite. They think themselves into a certain state and their world reinforces it, which encourages them to consider themselves even more worthy, or unworthy, to match their thoughts.

## The Law of Reciprocity

We all seek happiness, but it is not a destination to which we head for in anticipation of what we will receive when we arrive there. Rather, it is an ongoing state of being, dictated by our emotions. Knowing what makes us happy is a prerequisite to being happy because no one else can make us happy or provide happiness for us. It is an internal state that fluctuates daily, according to how we feel about ourselves – our level of self-esteem, in particular, the degree being strictly controlled by our capacity to give. When we give little of ourselves (little joy, little love, little time, little commitment) we receive little in return – the clear and unequivocal Law of Reciprocity. But if we have happiness, those we love can share in it, enhance it or strengthen its foundations while boosting our self-esteem. Happiness comes from knowing who we are and being ourselves, not from trying to impress or living in a dishonest way.

If we meet the ideal soulmate, and we don't know what will make us happy, how can he/she contribute to its enhancement? Happiness becomes elusive when we have none in the first place because there is nothing for anyone else to share. We then depend on finding someone to *make* us happy, to make us laugh or to uplift us. In short, to provide it all for us in a selfish way – only to rapidly discover that we cannot produce something from nothing. Happiness gained that way is false and transitory and also comes at a high cost. It means that without the other person's presence, we will always feel inadequate and most unhappy!

So how do you discover your own happiness? Simple enough. You do it through the 10 steps outlined in this book, especially steps one to five.

And we begin those steps by asking you a fundamental question: Just who do you think you are?

## Who ARE You?

How would you answer that question? Would you be The Manager from IT? The Jewish Rabbi? The Housewife from Hockley? The Director from Doncaster? The budding Rock Singer? Someone's Mother, Father, Sister, Child? The Muslim Imam? The Clever One? The Thin One? The African Caribbean Woman or The Chinese Shopkeeper? The list is obviously endless depending on your terms of reference, your values and your personal aspirations.

Whatever you cling to as your main 'handle' tells you where you are in your life, your perception of yourself and where you are going. Knowing exactly what you are about is crucial to your interaction with others and the quality of your life. Establishing your unique identity is essential for the respect you seek and what you actually receive in return. If someone values a prince and you perceive yourself a mere pauper, that person is certainly not for you. Or if she loves Bach and you like only punk music, there's a huge gap there to be bridged.

It is clear that names, titles and labels are the biggest indicators of our identity and what we value in ourselves. That's why we prize them so much. Mine is an 'empowering agent' and it says much about where I am going. You only have to look at some of the user names people choose on the Internet, or for their email addresses, to see how they regard themselves. Negative names like MonkeyMan, UglySister, OldCodger, Don'tHurtMe, FantasticLover etc., are in abundance. By the way, if you're wondering why that last name was included, it's because it takes two to create 'fantastic' love!

Such names send the loudest messages of how their owners perceive themselves and their expanding emotional baggage, i.e. they possess very low levels of confidence and self esteem. And it won't get better either. Pulling up that person's self-esteem will be hard work for his/her soulmate.

Often, when we do not know who we are, we hang on like puppets to recycled social labels that derive mainly from work roles that confirm us; or names from family and friends that have been foisted upon us since childhood, or labels associated with success or failure. We often don't stop to ask if that label really represents who we are, and wish to be for the rest of our lives. Names are always flexible according to where we are in time, but positive names and descriptions suggest people who are going places, not stuck in a rut.

So, what is *your* 'handle'?


## Culture and Gender References

Our identity is always culture- and gender-referenced, and tied to our aspirations. If you ask me who I am, I can easily tell you now, and with some smugness, though it wasn't like that a few years ago. That is because my own pattern of interaction has changed dramatically.

"I am Elaine Sihera, the best empowerment agent in my Universe, aiming to make a difference to others in whatever way possible. A loving, caring, competent, creative and talented woman with a winning smile; one who values mutual respect. One who is independent, who enjoys her own company, who revels in the beauty and possibilities of life and is most happy and contented just being herself. I feel fantastic at my age and am even looking forward to being older. I believe that I am a remarkable human being, reflecting the power and beauty of my Universe."

With such a positive outlook I would wish to interact in a positive way. Notice that my definition straddles three key elements of life: myself, my talents and my relationship with others. Definitions that focus only upon the self tend to leave a bitter taste of regret when they are finally realised. They have little impact on others, thus resulting in us feeling frustrated and insignificant. We are often left wondering whether we could have done something more fulfilling with our lives.

Conversely, definitions that push the self into the background and focus only upon service to others ultimately leave a feeling of resentment and being taken for granted, especially when we get little appreciation in return. Finally, definitions that say nothing about our own skills leave us feeling inadequate, and always comparing ourselves to others in a useless and futile effort to confirm our low self-worth.

My description reflects not only how I view myself, but it also does something even more powerful: it sends out a hidden message of what I actually WANT in a partner. Certain key words stand out either as a warning or a welcome to others: words like 'independent', 'competent' and 'loving', as well as my desire to be accepted as I am, not what someone else would like me to be.

In a nutshell, I am happy in my own skin as a successful, optimistic individual who likes my space and has high levels of confidence and self-esteem. My description suggests that I am seeking someone to enhance that feeling while I add to theirs, in whatever positive way they view themselves, so long as the chemistry is there.

## Desire for Approval

Do I care whether anyone agrees with my defi-nition/label or not? Heck, no! Not at all. I am not seeking approval or using anyone else's yard-stick to judge myself because I might not agree with how they perceive their world, either culturally or emotionally. I am judging myself by my own standards and values – the only standards and values that matter in my world.

Someone who feels troubled by my perspective, who does not consider me as 'one of us', who feels overwhelmed by my confident outlook, who thinks I might be too 'arrogant' in self-perception, or who does not share my aspirations of making that difference, would not be right for me as a partner. And I can usually work that out in the first few moments of a conversation! This could be why I have had only three main soulmates in my life so far, each relationship lasting a significant period of time. I can safely say that, for most of the time, they were all fantastic.

In fact, ever since I have decided who I am it has been reinforced almost word for word – especially the words 'loving' and 'remarkable' – by most of the people I interact with. Better still, my Universe keeps providing opportunities for me to use my skills to realise my main goal of making that difference. At times, it is quite amazing to see the way my self-belief is affirmed by others, by my environment and by my achievements.

So long as we do not seek to either hurt or offend others, we can have a field day deciding whom we wish to be and living as that person.  A desire for constant approval and a fear of upsetting others often prevent us living our lives in our own way. It stops us from acknowledging our true selves and taking great pride and pleasure in the unique beings we are.

## Noticing the Early Signs

The signs are ALWAYS there at the very first inter-action as to whether a couple will match or not. Often we deliberately ignore them because we are either trying to impress too much, we fear rejection, we are feeling desperate to find *anyone* because we are lonely or our body clock is ticking faster than ever, or we have a need to confirm that we are not being too picky and expecting perfection.

However, there is nothing picky about having firm values and standards that match your personality and then sticking to them. While you can compromise on certain lower order values, you cannot compromise on your core ones! As long as you are not seeking perfection you can afford to be choosy. *10 Easy Steps To....Finding Your Ideal Soulmate!* helps you do that sensitively.

By the way, knowing who you are does not mean someone else's definition of you because each person's perception of you will be quite different. Each will define and label you according to what you mean to them, what they might want of you, the role you play or what they wish to project on to you, etc. That is why defining who you are is of such vital importance. Everyone gets a consistent message regarding whom you aspire to be and can treat you accordingly, in ways that enhance, affirm and reinforce that image.

No one can compensate for your lack of happiness so you have to first build that joyous feeling inside you before you can confidently engage with that special someone. Being a complete person means you also accept that your soulmate, being complete too, will have a former life that needs to be respected and celebrated. Not to be ignored, wished away, resented or a source of jealousy.

Self-knowledge is essential in the interactive

process so **knowing who you are and being yourself** is the very first crucial step. Otherwise you are just half a person needing completion and will gradually become co-dependent upon your partner. The relationship will then assume a claustrophobic air, becoming dogged by insecurity, jealousy, resentment, possessiveness and a desire for constant attention and/or control. In such circumstances the enjoyment soon evaporates and the relationship breaks.

~~~~~~~~~~~~~~~~~~~~~~~~~~~~~~~~~~~

## *Exercise One*

Who are you at this moment? Do you have any idea, or are you still confused and even afraid to think about it?

Rate the knowledge of your identity now using the key on page 41. Any doubts you have should result in a 6 or 7, and if you're stuck at a crossroads during a time of transition that would rate a 4 or 5. If you genuinely need to do the exercise overleaf, your rating should be between 1 and 3.

By the time you finish *10 Easy Steps To....Finding Your Ideal Soulmate!*, your responses to all 10 steps should provide a useful guide to your current level of preparation, which you can gradually improve in order to find the right person for you. To work out who you are, which is NOT your personality but the image you have of your total self, take your time to do the following:

A. Write down everything that comes to mind relating to what you are now and wish to be, no matter how grand or strange it seems.

B. Make a list of the most important ones for you.

C. From that list, select your TOP FIVE descriptions of how you see yourself.

## My Top Five Core Descriptions
......which I cannot compromise, are:

1.

2.

3.

4.

5.

You may compromise on the other labels but you CANNOT compromise these top five core descriptions in any relationship because they represent the essence of you. No matter what you do, you really wouldn't be happy at all in the long term. You would be merely repressing the natural you to please someone else and you will always feel inadequate, or lack something vital in your life.

~~~~~~~~~~~~~~~~~~~~~~~~~~~~~~~~~~~

## REFLECTION

Step One in *Finding Your Ideal Soulmate*....

### KNOW WHO YOU ARE & BE YOURSELF!

....Others will know where you are coming from and how to treat you appropriately. Most importantly, they will know whether they can be of real value to you on the next stage of your personal journey.

✳ ✳ ✳ ✳ ✳ ✳

*You'll discover that real love is millions of miles past falling in love with anyone or anything. When you make that one effort to feel compassion instead of blame or self-blame, the heart opens again and continues opening.*

Sara Paddison

# ~ STEP TWO ~

## <u>Know What You Want</u>

Do you find it easy to know what you want and to express it clearly? If not, what is holding you back? Whether we pay homage to God, Nature, the Universe or whatever, there comes a time when we seek help or intervention for something important to us, something that relates to our innermost desires. Very often our prayers or requests are not granted and then we tend to lose hope. But we are not likely to have our prayers answered for three main reasons.

Firstly, we tend to pray or make our request when there is a crisis, so we pray with anxiety and desperation, with the panic button at full throttle. We have lots of doubts and fears, and with no real belief in routine miracles or in getting a result! Surprise, surprise, when nothing much happens, it then confirms the lurking doubt within us that our god doesn't truly care or isn't even there! Secondly, any prayer to a higher unseen power requires a massive leap of faith in what is possible and we tend to lack such blind faith.

Thirdly, and most importantly, we often fail to ask specifically for what we want because we have not stopped to think about it clearly. Instead we cling to a generalised idea of our situation – a broad "help me please!" plea – because too many things in our life might need sorting. We are also afraid to make our request specific in case it might seem unrealistic, unreasonable or even selfish to others. But that attention to specifics is what helps to provide focus, and once we start to focus we begin to energise the desire, to make it an intention rather than just a fleeting wish, which then moves people and our environment to help us to achieve it.

In fact, to show how the Universe delivers when we have faith, just think deeply on any item, like a model and colour of car, and focus upon it for a while. From that moment on, a rush of cars conforming to that model and colour will come into your vision, seeming to appear every-where. Articles which draw your attention in newspapers and magazines are likely to relate to it while a number of unexpected occur-rences connected to that model of car will begin to happen.

The power of thought is phenomenal when it comes to fulfilling our wishes. Sooner or later, circumstances will conspire in a series of 'coinci-dences' to give us that car, if it was our desire. We are on earth to be happy and healthy; to have our desires fulfilled. However, it is a focus on negativity that keeps us feeling unhappy, unfulfilled, constantly ill or sometimes in despair.

## The Power of Thought and Belief

There is no great mystery to fulfilling our dreams. So long as we can articulate exactly what we want, we can always achieve it with action and commitment. I am in total agreement with Steve Andreas and Charles Faulkner (*NLP: The New Technology of Achievement*[2]) when they write, "In NLP we believe that anyone can do anything. If it's not possible the world of experience will let us know. We'll find out by doing, not by thinking that we can't." In fact, I believe that we can have anything we want in our lives if we have five simple attributes, which I call my 'magical ingredients':

1. The **SELF-BELIEF** that we can make it happen.

2. The **FAITH** in our abilities, or in a higher power, to carry it out.

3. The **ACTION** and effort to bring it to being.

4. The willingness to pay the price in focus and **COMMITMENT**

5. The **COURAGE** and patience to see it through.

There is nothing so strange about my suggestion because it is the power of thought and belief that has built our world. When I use my computer, and the Internet, I am writing and researching on someone else's thought that they brought into being through sheer belief, regardless of who might have told them it was a crass idea which would never work.

When I use a microwave, I use someone else's thought, the direct manifestation of his/her faith in what is possible. I remember the fear around radiation that was prevalent when we first started using it, which seems such a long time ago now! When I drive my car I am thankful to Henry Ford's thought and experimentation for both my comfort and journey. When I turn on my radio, I am able to enjoy my music and the news through Marconi's belief in radio waves, the very same beliefs that had him put away in a mental hospital for being 'mad'!

Every time I turn on the electric light that we take so much for granted I am using Thomas Edison's thought and the personal courage and determination that took him 10,000 attempts and a massive leap of faith to bring it into being.

And, as you read my book, you are sharing my thought and creation, the end result and confirmation of a deep faith and belief that I could actually write a book for public consumption, take action on it and find the courage and determination to bring it to life! Like all those people I mentioned, I simply asked, believed in it, took action and it was given. Experience, and lots of achievements, has taught me that every thought and creation is marked by eight stages:

**1. Excitement**    **2. Fear**
**3. Possibility**    **4. Belief**

**5. Faith**          **6. Action**

**7. Commitment**     **8. Result**

With any new idea, everyone feels a sense of excitement at what is possible. However, most people get stuck on stage two (**Fear**) and so very little happens to them to reinforce the talent and ability they know they possess. I have few fears so I get a result EVERY TIME, even if it is not the result I wanted. That only fires me up to keep trying until I get the desired outcome. There is nothing more exciting than creating your own reality, seeing an idea take life from nothing except your thought, and then watching it evolve to something tangible. Others might get past stage two but only reach stage three (**Possibility**) in their ideas and still end up doing nothing.

A few might even make it to stage six (**Action**), but still lack the stickability to produce the right results, while the ones who have the five essential elements mentioned earlier (my magical ingredients) will triumph in the end. They will get a result, no matter how long it takes. **If you believe it, you can create it.** Your focus and thought processes will eventually find the means and resources to do it and your commitment will give it life. This applies particularly to finding the right soulmate. If you believe someone special is there for you, your faith, action and commitment will bring him into your world. It's your level of resistance, scepticism and non-belief that will keep her away.

## Getting the Desired Results

Self-belief and faith are two powerful tools in getting us what we require, but without the action to bring it to life, and the courage and commitment to stick with it and see it through, we will always remain dreamers. Self-belief and faith separate dreamers from achievers because they are governed by our past experiences. If we have not done very well in our own eyes so far, or have not achieved the success we have sought, both of these ingredients gradually diminish as we brand ourselves 'failures' and hide behind our fears.

We eventually come to dread trying and experimenting with anything new because we fear having to face the consequences of any actions that fail to live up to expectations. But consequences are a key part of results, we cannot escape them. The only way to cope with them is to get more of the kind of results we desire through belief, application and commitment to that belief.

You might be surprised to hear that there is no such thing as 'failure' or 'success'. Rather, these are powerful labels that we choose to put on the RESULTS that flow from our actions, and we can always change our results by merely changing those actions. Results show us what works and what doesn't, or what is absent from our learning and our information. As Edison said, every 'failed' attempt was not a failure. It merely showed him one more way that didn't work!

It is FEAR that prevents us from knowing what we want or becoming achievers because fear paralyses our efforts and actions and stops our desired results dead in their tracks. Our need for affirmation ensures that we often believe others might ridicule our cherished desires; that they might think we are not worthy or competent enough to fulfil them; that they might compare us to themselves and find us wanting or that they might discourage us from achieving our desires. So we stop in fear while our desires remain as dreams.

In fact, it is the people we most value who often loom large in our imagination, waiting smugly to tell us "I told you so!" and, in the face of that perception, we cease to try. As we seek approval from such significant others as parents, siblings, relatives, friends, soulmates and work colleagues, we deny those specific dreams and think in generalised terms instead, not daring to hope that our life could change; that it could become exactly how we desire it. But, under those circumstances, which are dogged by fear, nothing much will happen.

Unless you dream in specific terms, and have the faith and commitment to match, you cannot utilise the five magical ingredients that are necessary for goal realisation. Worst of all, if you don't know what you want, you won't know it when you actually see it!

## The Consequences of Ignorance

We have lots of needs every day which is by deliberate design to keep us growing and our world evolving. But we will not be happy with what we get unless it coincides exactly with, or is very close to, what we actually want. Knowing what we want is thus essential to getting it and nowhere is this more relevant than in finding a soulmate.

We really need to know what we want in a potential spouse or partner because, once we are settled with her/him, the little things we didn't want will be popping their heads out to annoy and mock us. Those little gremlins we feared will be having a field day at our expense. Hence the famous warning: "Marry in haste, repent at leisure!"

If you go by looks alone when you meet him, later on when he leaves his clothes lying around the nice, neat house, or goes to golf every weekend when you would like him with you at home (or somewhere else), it won't be very jolly or the least bit romantic! Men who visit nightclubs to drink and watch people dance, without dancing themselves, are good examples of those who do not really know what they want.

They hope to find a soulmate in this loud and noisy environment, full of gyrating bodies. Yet many are not dancers and perhaps don't even like dancing. Rather, they seem content to stare at the dancers all night, while downing as many pints as possible – seemingly to gain Dutch courage – which, in turn, makes them even less attractive. The pub would have been a far more suitable place, but they do not care to be in a pub. They prefer to be 'near the action'.

However, should they find a suitable woman in this environment, once the relationship is underway, she is likely to want to go dancing in the future. If he doesn't feel like going to the club with her, which is very likely, he will resent her going with her friends or on her own! As dancing might represent a core activity for his partner, this would not be such an easy issue to resolve.

## The Search for Perfection

A friend once asked me, "How do you know what you want until you see it?" That is a fair question, especially when one is young and inexperienced. That is why I suggested that this book would be more suitable for those in their mid-20s and over, who have already experimented. Everyone has to practise until they know what suits them. But often we are used to doing something out of habit and it is not until we sample something else that we realise what we are missing. For many people, trial and error and word of mouth decide what they want in life. It doesn't matter how you discover it, once you are aware of what really makes you happy you can always add new experiences to it, but you cannot compromise it.

Knowing what you want is not prescriptive, if it concerns important elements that would irritate, annoy or put you off. It is essential for your well-being. For example, desiring someone of a certain religion, profession, culture or skill is important because most people are judged by those aspects in society. But ruling out an individual because of the newspaper they read, their eye colour or hair colour (which can easily be changed these days) is nitpicking! These kinds of things do not make the person. They might suggest a certain type of individual but they are mere indicators of direction, not the route itself.

Focusing only upon trivial external things does not suggest that you know what you really want. Rather, it suggests a desire for perfection in your

choice of companion caused by your own inse-
curities and doubts. The best approach is one
that safeguards your core values and activities
but leaves your mind open to see what kind of
person matches them. Balance is really important in any kind of choice and often it comes in
the most unexpected form – like David was for
me. The skill here is to allow for the possibility by
being flexible.


## Overly Prescriptive Types

At the other end of the choice range are the
overly-prescriptive types: people who are
seeking soulmates but have already decided
which place abroad they are going to live or
when they will be sailing round the world, for
example – the kind of decisions which should be
made by *both* parties. In fact, one man came
back to Britain on a Monday from Spain to
specifically search for a woman whom he
believed would drop everything she was doing
that week (strewth!) and go with him to live
permanently in Spain. He expected to be flying

70                                    *10 Easy Steps To....*

back with his prized catch the following Saturday!

He had barely a week to make the biggest decision of his life, find her, and take her back with him, but that worried him none. Perhaps, in his perception, most women would simply be sitting down filing their nails waiting for such a proposal. He didn't give a reason for this undue haste but he expected his wish to materialise, asking me if I were interested, and adding how much he would 'pamper' me too. No, I wasn't. I had a book to write instead! He knew what he wanted, yes, but in order to achieve his wish he was prepared to infringe upon someone else's right by forcing them into a decision in an unreasonable time period.

His wish is likely to be granted, in view of his determination, but he is likely to pay dearly for it at some point. In such a short time, he is unlikely to select someone who is truly compatible with him. He is likely to find a woman who is only interested in his money or the main chance. That will gradually, and painfully, reveal itself in the later months.

One has to wonder whether such people live in the real world. But they do, and they are called controllers, especially if they believe money can buy them anything in life.

**<u>Stop here</u>** and rate the knowledge of your desires out of 10. Do you REALLY know what you want from your life at this moment? Any specific or major things? Better still, do you know what five essential things you must have in a partner? The rest can come as a surprise, but what are these core requirements?

## The Power of Values

The most important thing in knowing what we want comes from our values. Once we work out the values we have for our life (like happiness, security, joy, love, respect, etc.), finding the ideal soulmate becomes highly probable through discovering someone who aligns with most of those core values.

For example, if you are a lawyer and are proud of it and you choose to match up with someone who neither likes nor respects lawyers, or who makes a joke out of your skill, then you will always be justifying or defending one of the things you care most about – your livelihood and profession. That is not a good way to start a relationship as you are immediately at a clear disadvantage. You and your soulmate should be proud of the careers you have both chosen in order to give each other the necessary support and encouragement in the relationship.

In the last years of my marriage, after some trial and error, I discovered what I wanted for myself as a life-long profession: to recognise achievers through the annual awards I created. It did not give me much money, as I hoped for in a business, but it was extremely satisfactory and enriching in other ways, especially affecting the life of others in such a positive way. It also gave me many new skills (like business management, writing and publishing) and rewards I never expected, particularly the impact I have been making on my community. However, my idea was not really supported by my partner at any point in my new journey, which made the venture needlessly hard.

The lack of adequate income also caused a nagging resentment and much argument very often. In those situations, either the activity has to go or the relationship eventually collapses from the strain of the lack of support and difference in opinion. Sadly, the marriage went in the end as I found it difficult to give up what my heart wanted me to do and thus made my choice.


## Giving up Things for Love

We can only enjoy our lives and feel fulfilled by being true to ourselves, and that is possible only through the alignment of our values with both the ideal and the reality. If we believe one thing yet live by another, we are like caricatures of what we seek, dwelling in pretence, constant frustration, resentment of others, unhappiness and a lack of self-love.

Sadly, sometimes knowing what we want does not mean that others are going to take any notice of it. In Jackie's dating profile she has been clear about wanting someone 'single, slim and a non-smoker'. She said that she even put the words in block capitals to ensure that they stand out. Yet the number of men who weighed at least 17 stones, were 'occasional' smokers and were very much married who sent her messages left her wondering which bit of 'slim, single and non-smoker' did they not understand! Obviously, the slim, elegant image of their bodies in their heads bore no relation to the ones Jackie saw in their photographs!

Some men also offered to 'give up smoking' for her – BAD idea – especially as, for most, that would be one of their core values! They would soon start smoking again when she was 'in the bag' because they would not be giving it up for themselves, but using it as a dispensable means to a desired end.

Knowing what you want also needs to be 'realistic' but, as Anthony Robbins said in *Unlimited Power*[3], being realistic has never invented anything nor achieved anything spectacular. We have to think outside the box for that sort of achievement; to dare to dream the unthinkable and to wish for the impossible, as illustrated by the next heartwarming story.

On returning from a holiday I met a very happy couple on the plane, Nita and Paresh, who had been married for nine years and yet behaved like newly-weds. When I asked how they met, he proceeded to tell me their interesting story. She was a qualified doctor and he a mere student when they met at a reception in

London. He knew instantly that he wanted to marry her but she was sceptical and kept ignoring him. He knew her parents and when he expressed that wish to them, they told him bluntly that he couldn't afford her and he should look elsewhere!

## Achieving the Impossible

Undaunted, he kept engineering meetings to see Nita whenever she went out, and kept on wishing, hoping and working, while patiently gaining her confidence and trust. Within three years he actually proposed. He said that money was not the real obstacle to their union. Instead, it was the whole package relating to her and the challenge of her being in 'another league' from him. Paresh was determined to prove he was worthy because he wanted no one else, and he got his wish in the end.

Their story shows that dreams can be as real-istic, or as impossible, as we wish them to be, so long as we have the five magical ingredients to make them happen. Paresh certainly had the self-belief and faith in himself to win over his love. He took action to work his way upwards on the career ladder toward her. He remained focused and committed for three years, never feeling discouraged or losing sight of his goal. He also had the courage and the patience to see it through to claim the prize.

He was smiling all the way through the story, as if it were a great challenge he had overcome. As he said, he knew what he wanted and was determined to get it, if Nita wanted him too, and he knew she liked him from the first moment they met. She just needed convincing of his commitment.

Knowing what we want is a passport to the soulmate we would like to meet, to the life we would like to lead and to the kind of person we wish to develop into. Imagine going into a shop with all kinds of life achievements, where you can have anything you want. An assistant is waiting patiently to select the items you wish for, because you cannot have everything you see, and you have only 15 minutes to make your choices.

What are you going to choose? Or are you going to dither until the 15 precious minutes have passed, leaving you with nothing? Only you can answer that question. But making use of an opportunity through knowing what we want means we will never be short of opportunities to realise our dreams.

~~~~~~~~~~~~~~~~~~~~~~~~~~~~~~~~

### *Exercise Two*

So what exactly do you desire in your soulmate at this moment? What are you prepared to accept in other parts of your life? The simple exercise below should give you a much better idea.

  A. *Write down three headers: Personal, Relationship and Professional (Work). Under each category, list as many things you can think of that you desire.*

For example, the Personal section might describe your aspirations for a car, a house, a holiday in some faraway place, etc.. The Relationship section might have your desire for someone articulate, charming, humorous, independent, etc.. Anything at all that comes to mind, write it down, no matter how trivial or unusual it might seem.

  B. *Select your TOP FIVE requirements from the items in each category.*

*10 Easy Steps To....*

You will be able to see at a glance the main desires you have across the three most essential areas of your life. If you start focusing upon them, writing them down in detail, visualising them clearly each day and living as though they are already in your reach, especially using the magical ingredients, they will slowly begin to materialise. Try it on at least one desire and see!

My main requirements of any potential soul-mate, in priority order, is that there must be mutual *physical attraction* and *chemistry*, *respect*, *love*, *communication* and *support*. If my soulmate does not demonstrate all or most of those requirements, we are not going to get very far. But everything else is negotiable. In fact, I had all of those at the beginning of my marriage. By the end of it only the physical attraction was left – not much on which to sustain a relationship with someone.

For work, *writing*, *creating*, *communicating*, *empowering* and *instructing* are right at the top. It means that, if my work does not contain ALL or most of those elements, I cannot be happy as I would be prevented from expressing those talents in myself and would always feel frustrated and dissatisfied.

As I said before, you CANNOT compromise your top five core requirements in a relationship because they represent the essence of you. No matter what you do, you really wouldn't be happy at all in the long-term, as you would be repressing the natural you to please someone else. You will always feel inadequate or lack something vital in your life.

*10 Easy Steps To....Finding Your Ideal Soulmate!* should identify the route to achieving that goal and guide you purposefully on it.

~~~~~~~~~~~~~~~~~~~~~~~~~~~~~~~~~~~

## REFLECTION

Step Two in *Finding Your Ideal Soulmate....*

## *KNOW WHAT YOU WANT!*

.... You will be able to spot it more easily, you will achieve it with less difficulty and others will be in no doubt as to whether they too can provide it or not. Most importantly, it avoids unintended slight, rejection or misunderstanding in your search or in other key areas of your life.

# ~ STEP THREE ~

## <u>Know What You Stand For & Where You're Heading</u>

I have never been a member of a political party but I don't sit on the fence or hog the middle of the road either. My mother used to tell me that people who sit on fences are very precarious and only get sore bums! I try to remember that often. I know precisely what I stand for and none of the parties yet reflect it. Furthermore, many politicians expect you to accept their words as evidence of their sincerity. However, I do not judge people by their words or intention, only by their deeds – and it takes a while for these to emerge.

I also have deep negative feelings about the word 'empire' and so have steered clear of it in any connection with civic honours I could have received. It means I might have lost out on public acclaim on one superficial level, but I know who I am and what my principles are on the other. They are priceless to my identity and sense of value.

So where are you at this moment? Firmly on one side of the road, or hovering uncomfortably in the middle of it as vehicles career around you? Are you falling for one idea or another, depending upon convenience? It really matters to have an opinion on life and to speak up for yourself, not just for someone else. At least others know where you are coming from and where you wish to go. On the one hand, they can respect you for it and perhaps even help you to get there.

Alternatively, they might not like what you are saying, but they will know your alignment and have a clearer understanding of you. It is also about trust. If people are not sure of you, it will be difficult to gain their trust as they are likely to believe that you might be disapproving, superficial, hypocritical or disloyal. Marking your spot very clearly is a sign of confidence and a leader, and, when it comes to relationships, it takes on an even greater significance.

I spent at least 20 years of my life constantly having to defend my beliefs in thinly-disguised 'discussions' within my marriage because my partner was drawn to one political party and I to another which were diametrically opposite in ethos! Being young, and caring only about love and romance, I did not know who I was when I met my soulmate or what I really stood for when I got married. But I would have a long, some-times painful, time finding out.

## The Importance of Belief

Before you meet anyone, you need to know what you stand for and where you are going. Only then can you compare these core values to the principles of your soulmate to identify the degree of alignment, or the width of the gap, which is likely to exist between you both. Beliefs are not trivial things. They are anchors to our development. Our beliefs are fundamental to how we see ourself, or see one another; how we perceive our close family and friends and the world itself. This in turn dictates our actions.

However, beliefs are never static. They are constantly changing according to new experiences and challenges.

Beliefs also affect others because they control every interaction. If you believe, for instance, that a work colleague is smarter, brighter or better than you are, you will always behave in an inferior way to match it, or possibly with envy and resentment, whenever you see or interact with that person. This perception gradually becomes a self-fulfilling prophesy because you will be suiting action to belief in every single meeting, without even being aware of it!

The same with your beliefs regarding finding a partner. If you think there is no one out there good enough for you, sure enough you will find no one who matches up to you because people will sense your very high standards and shy away from meeting them. They will feel overwhelmed by the idea of even trying to measure up to this impossible ideal you expect. Result: your expectations are proved right!

You cannot compromise beliefs by being vague and dithery or being too strong and negative. You need to show who you are positively, what you want, what you stand for and where you are heading, while at the same time allowing for some flexibility in your expectation and development. It means that you will take only those who want to go with you, or you'll soften a little to align with them, and leave the rest, while being prepared for the unexpected.

People also worry about not meeting the 'right' person, believing that they need tons of potential mates to choose from. But, just like winning the lottery from only one line of play, it takes only one person to be THE one, no more. That's all we need for a long-lasting relationship. One person, who loves, cares and wants to share our lives. So don't be put off by those who do not value your principles and direction.

So long as your values are realistic and positive, and you are not too prescriptive and immovable, cultivating the people who like you as you are will prove far more rewarding, exciting and enriching than worrying about those who do not.

## Pleasing Yourself First

It was Bill Cosby, the American comedian, who

said, "I do not know the secret of success, but the secret of failure is trying to please too many people all the time."

I live by that tenet daily.

You cannot please everyone you interact with, so the safest place to start is to please yourself. Those who like what you do will be for you and those who don't will reveal themselves too and that shouldn't concern you too much. If such people dislike you for one thing, you are unlikely to be accepted for anything else, so save your efforts.

When you love yourself you have to accept that not everyone will love you too and then live with that knowledge. Knowing what you stand for is also the surest way to gain the appreciation, value and respect you seek because people will approach you favourably or retreat accordingly. That should help you to understand your interactions better and use them to your best advantage in achieving your objectives. Above all, you will earn respect as someone who can't be bought.

It is fear and emotional insecurity that cause us to wait on others to set the pace before revealing what we wish for or stand for. But doors always open wide for the person who knows where he is going and how she is going to get there. It is true that some doors do not open instantly, that some might take their time, but they do open in the end to let the fearless through.

Knowing what you stand for also means that you will be exposed to more like-minded and encouraging people, kindred spirits who will be there to support you on your journey. People who don't understand you are likely to make assumptions about you, often wrongly, to judge you negatively and then ignore you. That is fine. You can do without those types on your journey.


If you feel frustrated most times in getting your point across or expressing yourself adequately, it is because you are in the wrong job or living with the wrong kind of people who are not affirming what you believe or reinforcing you as you are. Life then becomes an endless competition or a steep uphill battle as you struggle to be heard, or have to shout over others to do so. We cannot shine unless we are affirmed because it is feeling valued that gives meaning and purpose to life.

The foundation of what we stand for is our

values, those key elements that control our perception of the world and our behaviour. Values are supremely important, the "measuring sticks of life", according to the NLP creators. What we value determines what life means to us, i.e what decisions we will make, what actions we will take and whether we will, in general, approach or avoid new challenges. It means values cannot be ignored. For example, if you are someone who likes a challenge, then your set of values might include adventure, courage, the search for excellence, self-reliance, learning, self-development, solving problems and stimulating change.

But would your new partner appreciate such values if he/she knew about them in advance? Are you living without such opportunities in your life now? How do you feel if you are? Would your soulmate want you being too adventurous if their values set embraces safety, security, comfort, contentment, order, reliability and unchanging permanence?

Someone is bound to feel frustrated in such a partnership if they do not get the chance to live according to their own values and beliefs. And it is usually the weaker, more fearful, person who loses out in that kind of mismatch.

Finding Your Ideal Soulmate!

## The Origins of Values

Your values are the sets of feelings that let you know what is important to you. Every time you feel good about doing something in your life, or feel excited at the prospect of it (like the feeling I get when I am writing a book), you are fulfilling a value that means a lot to you. Values come originally from your parents, then from your peer group and then through your workplace, from the people you routinely try to impress. Finally, they come from yourself through increased awareness and knowledge.

What a lot of people subconsciously deny is that they can actually change their values and thus their lives, dramatically. But not only can values change in an instant, they also change as we grow, and become more aware of our aspirations and identity. So long as we are flexible, anything is possible.

You might not be aware of this, but every behaviour you exhibit is either to avoid pain or to receive pleasure, depending upon your individual value system. If you are reluctant to change your values it is likely that you associate pain with them (the pain of disapproval, of isolation from a significant person or group, of punishment, of guilt, of disappointment or of confused identity, to name a few examples). So there is always a hidden, or an open, reason for your actions. If you are not sure what your values are, there are two ways of finding out.

The first is to think back to when you were last annoyed or angry with someone. What triggered it? What exactly caused you to feel annoyed? By asking yourself these questions about all your disagreements you will be able to identify which of your values were being violated at the time.

When my ex-husband and I used to discuss our political views, he would often scoff at my opinions. At that point I always felt that he was violating my values of autonomy and the freedom to think as I choose. No doubt he perceived that I violated similar values relating to him, hence the continued mutual irritation.

✳ ✳ ✳ ✳ ✳ ✳

*A man can fail many times, but he isn't a failure until he begins to blame somebody else.*

John Burroughs

## Living Against Your Values

The second way to assess personal values is to imagine events that fulfil your needs and make you feel good. It could be someone inviting you to a concert, which might fulfil your values of respect, appreciation and love of music. If you enjoy events like that, it means they reflect those values you cherish. That is why when we value something but ignore it, or suppress it in our life, we are bound to come unstuck at some point because we are not being true to ourselves. Whenever we are frustrated in our achievement, a value is usually the culprit blocking our progress, because it might be incompatible with what we actually desire, or perhaps we have too readily compromised or repressed it!

Not being true to oneself generates unnecessary mental conflict and anguish. For example, we might value one thing – like honesty – but secretly have affairs, or slag off our friends and colleagues behind their backs, and then wonder why there is no trust at home or why we have so few friends!

If we are also stuck in an unfulfilling job which goes against our values of self-fulfilment and job satisfaction, and which puts a salary at the heart of everything, we will continue to be unhappy, lack self-esteem and underachieve. Worst of all, if we are stuck in an unhappy relationship, yet do nothing about it, we are living in conflict with our values and will always be unhappy until we find the courage to change it.


Because values give us both purpose and meaning, success becomes elusive when we don't know exactly where we are heading and what our purpose is. Many people achieve short-term aims, like money, status or even soul-mates, but still remain largely unhappy and unfulfilled because of living in a way which is out of synch with their values. It is thus important to be sure of your values and beliefs before you search for your soulmate. You can negotiate with yourself around certain beliefs, but every change of value and belief threatens your very identity and the foundation that forms your personality. For that reason we are always resistant to any request for changes within us and certainly won't do so at the drop of a hat.

We tend to alter our values only when we believe that the change will not only enhance and benefit us, but we also have nothing to lose by doing so. We don't change because someone else suggests it. In fact, that is the time we will stick to that belief or value just to be obstinate and prove ourselves independent!

Neither do we get change from others by browbeating or nagging them into it. Rather, we actually have to change their belief system first, which in turn shifts their values as they gradually come to see, clearly, that the suggested change in attitude or behaviour is not only the right thing to do, but also highly beneficial for them.

## Changing From Within

With all that in mind, the next time that you go looking for a soulmate, if you believe she is too fat or too thin, too common or too posh, leave her alone. Don't try to change her to fit your ideal unless she initiates the change. Otherwise it will work only for the brief time that she is trying to impress you. Sure enough, she will go on all sorts of weight reduction/improvement diets, and might even try elocution lessons, because the excitement of the new relationship will encourage her to do anything for you. However, soon after you have settled down and she feels secure, the weight will be back on, or she will still be swearing like a trouper, because you did not change her belief system and she certainly did not change it for herself.

Again, if you see a guy who smokes or drinks too much, who is a workaholic or is sports mad, and those are values which conflict with your own, leave him alone too. Things will NOT change after you are married or living together, contrary to popular belief. He might cut down on what he likes, or even stop briefly, in order to impress you, and to show you his sincerity and commitment. However, that is likely to lead to resentment and animosity when he misses those activities and then starts to re-establish his old lifestyle in order to live harmoniously within himself. Worst still, he will also blame you for the wretched way he feels, which won't help his mood or feelings toward you.

The best advice is always to be who you are, and to love yourself for your identity and your principles. Have sincere values and beliefs but ensure that you are also open to other differing values and beliefs. However, don't compromise your values for your soulmate, otherwise you will always be leading someone else's life, perhaps in a state of bewilderment, confusion and resentment. Try not to be closed to change either. If you can see the reason and logic behind it, then you should give change a try, or give a little in expectations. But it must be done willingly and with a belief in its value to YOU.

Knowing what you stand for and where you are going might not impress the next woman you meet, but perhaps she is not meant for you anyway. In any doubtful situation, disregard your ego and desire to impress, say hello and goodbye – and walk on fast. The ideal soulmate who appreciates you as you are could be just around the next corner you take. Believe me, you won't have any trouble convincing her (or him) to finish the journey with you.

*10 Easy Steps To....*

~~~~~~~~~~~~~~~~~~~~~~~~~~~~~~~~~~

### *Exercise Three*

So, how much would you rate your knowledge of your principles and direction at this moment? Do you know what you really stand for, and are you prepared to defend it? What are your true values? The exercise below should help you to sort them out.

A. *On the next two pages are five sets of values. Place each set in order of importance to you. Which sets do you feel most comfortable with? Ignore the fact that some of the values (like Health and Success) could be placed in every set.*

B. *Go through each of the sets and select any words which truly reflect your outlook, needs and beliefs. Cross out the others.*

C. *Add any other value you might have that isn't listed. Whatever is left in front of you constitute your individual values that make you the person you are.*

D. *Finally, select 10 of the most important values and place them in priority order in the empty box provided. Your ideal soul-*

Finding Your Ideal Soulmate!

**A**

Adventure
Challenge
Courage
Excitement
Fearlessness
Fun
Learning
Problem-
solving
Wisdom
Travel
Analysis
Zest
Vitality

**B**

Comfort
Contentment
Order
Health
Safety
Security
Dignity
Elegance
Harmony
Loyalty
Service
Simplicity
Perseverance

**C**

Creativity
Innovation
Communication
Excellence
Fulfilment
Autonomy
Mastery
Self-Growth
Self-Reliance
Success
Joy
Wealth
Talent

**D**

Caring
Helping
Empowerment
Intimacy
Love
Happiness
Respect
Sharing
Trust
Humour
Contribution
Significance
Making a difference

**E**

Fairness
Justice
Change-agent
Personal Power
Freedom
Truth
Honesty
Evolution
Uniqueness
Merit
Diversity
Equality

*10 Easy Steps To....*

*mate would need to match, or contribute to the fulfilment of, all or most of the top five!*

Each of these sets of values reflects a certain type of person. **Set A** will be favoured by adventurers and those who welcome challenges, like Ellen MacArthur and Sir Ranulf Fiennes, as well as the analytical and investigative types; **Set B** will reflect those who do not welcome, or who react slowly to, change; those who emphasise traditions, service and loyalty – i.e the many civil servants who serve our country. They tend to be very good organisers and administrators.

**Set C** is indicative of entrepreneurs and innovators, people who are highly creative and independent in thought and action – like Richard Branson and Lord Moon – those who are most willing to take the risks. **Set D** reflects people who care unselfishly for others – social carers who devote their lives to positive interactions and making a difference to their world in a tangible way – Mother Teresa being an extreme example of this. **Set E** relates to people who would like to fix the world, those with a conscience for removing inequalities and ensuring justice – Mahatma Gandhi, Eleanor Roosevelt, Bob Marley and Martin Luther King Jr come easily to mind.

**My Priority Values are:**

1.
2.
3.
4.
5.
6.
7.
8.
9.
10.

Matching values to soulmates or jobs is thus very important. For example, if your values match Set C, then going into the uniformed services, which stress hierarchy, service and traditions, would not be good for your growth or sense of fulfilment. Or if you really like people and seek to empower their development, having the values of an adventurer (Set A), which mainly involves personal challenges for your own benefit, would

*10 Easy Steps To....*

not provide a solid foundation or the right environment for your mission.

My priority sets would have to be C, E and then D, and, to complement me, my ideal soulmate is likely to be found with values reflecting Set A or D. No doubt, David would choose Set C or A as his main one! My Top 10 values in priority order are: *Respect, Love, Creativity, Health, Fulfilment, Independence, Communication, Appreciation, Making a Difference* and *Spontaneity* as I dislike anything too regimented.

When we lack self-love and self-belief we usually attach ourselves to other people's values. But this seldom works because it gives little indication of what we are really about and makes us appear weak and dependent. We will also end up changing with the wind or sitting on the fence until we are swept away by the force of other people's principles!

Most importantly, this lack of firm personal values does not make us very attractive either. It is hoped that *10 Easy Steps To....Finding Your Ideal Soulmate!* will help you to identify those core values and make them work for you in every personal interaction.

~~~~~~~~~~~~~~~~~~~~~~~~~~~~~~~~~~

**REFLECTION**

Step Three in *Finding Your Ideal Soulmate*....

## KNOW WHAT YOU STAND FOR & WHERE YOU'RE HEADING!

.... You will take others with you more easily and you will establish your own standard and earn their respect. You will also identify the right soulmate for you. Better still, that soulmate is likely to have spotted you well beforehand!

❋ ❋ ❋ ❋ ❋ ❋

*Happiness resides not in possessions and not in gold, the feeling of happiness dwells in the soul.*

Democritus (460?-370? BC)

# ~ STEP FOUR ~

## <u>Chemistry: You Must Have It!</u>

One of the positive aspects of our long marriage was its chemistry. Even a few months before I left home we would still look at each other and want to smile and make love instantly. This was a marked continuation of the heady and youthful days we shared for the first few years when we were stuck like glue, virtually living in bed together! It was an incredible feeling of excitement and affirmation, being such a loving couple at the beginning – one of the major things that eroded when resentment and vindictiveness crept in.

In view of this, I have always found it fascinating seeing couples walking together, or in restaurants, for example, and how physically close they are, particularly how often they look at each other – the clearest pointers to the state of the relationship, and the value they place on one another. It can be very sad when a couple is sitting as if miles apart without saying a word, as this young couple did for over an hour after the first few words they said led to an obvious disagreement! Instead of leaving in order to address their differences and allow their expressions, they sat like unfeeling statues, not eating and avoiding eye contact, for an awfully long time. Clearly, a lack of chemistry on this date!

We constantly talk about 'chemistry', that elusive ingredient that binds us to one another, but no one is quite sure how it comes about. You might see someone you instantly recoil from, only to find that you fall in love with him soon afterwards, or that she gradually grows on you and alters your initial perception. Other times we meet people we believe we should instantly fall for, yet the friendship remains firmly on a platonic level. Like my friend, Tom, whom I befriended a few months after his wife died. We communicate very well, spending hours on the phone just chatting.

One Christmas day we talked for eight hours

non-stop (he about his wife, Barbara, and me about David), experiencing an uncontrollable flow of words which we seem unable to stem as we analysed, cogitated and gave insights into each other's lives. It felt good and satisfying to communicate on such an affirming level. Yet, while there is great warmth between us, there is no desire to make it intimate. It is just wonderful making this rare connection.

## Mutual Reinforcement

Many people complain about not being able to attract others or not being able to find that chemistry with a suitable partner. This could be because attraction is a reflection of mutual rein-forcement of the *whole* individual, not just the bits we like. This becomes a powerful force for personal empowerment, but it does not work unless we know what we are looking for or what to expect. Neither will it work if we are constantly finding fault or seeking perfection.

Where this force is very strong, there is much passion, much desire for intimacy and proximity and much longing to be as one. Where it is weak – because we are focusing more on what is lacking in the other person, or on the functionality and usefulness of the friendship – the attraction operates from a distance, on a platonic, business or casual level. But it still binds people in a mutually beneficial and enjoyable way.

As random as attraction might, at first, appear to be between two people, there is nothing random about it at all. It works on a complex level with definite rules. Attraction is primarily about possessing the qualities to satisfy five crucial factors in one another.

1. To fulfil the *needs* of others;
2. To make their experience more *pleasurable*;
3. To increase their level of *excitement*;
4. To enhance their feelings of *significance* and *value* (through appreciation and reinforcement);
5. To reduce their *emotional cost* of being involved with you (by enhancing the happiness factor.).

**Stop here** and rate the person in your life (or your

last relationship) out of 10 for each of these elements as you are receiving them NOW (or received them at the time). Then rate yourself on how you are providing (or have provided) these five elements to that person. Encourage your soulmate to complete it too.

What are the scores out of 50? Are they over 40 or under 20? How are you in both receiving and giving? Is there a big discrepancy between your score and that of your soulmate? Or between what you are giving and what you are receiving? This should be an illuminating exercise in the personal perceptions of both parties.

## Fulfilling the Needs of Others

The more you can provide those five core elements mentioned, the more attractive you will appear to your soulmate because the basis of attraction is looking outward to others. Some people never seem attractive enough, remaining single for long periods without any kind of attention or affirmation, finding it really difficult to keep others attracted. Or they have relationships that do not last very long. This tends to happen to people who lack self-love or are afraid of commitment; those unable to be open and honest, who lack generosity and find it difficult to give anything of themselves. In short, those who only care to receive because they are unsure how to give, or they put their needs above their partner's.

A key rule of thumb in the attraction process is that the more you focus upon yourself, the less attractive you will appear to others because you would not be reinforcing anyone else. Real attraction is about fulfilling the needs of others, not just worrying about your own. Attraction also begins with self-knowledge, particularly in knowing what pleases or irritates you. Other preferences come from experience, as we gradually associate certain things and people with positive feelings while resisting those who make us feel bad. However, because we are seldom sure of what we actually want, it cannot be reflected back to us.

Soon we begin to feel anxious that the date or relationship isn't working. The real problem is that our soulmate does not know what to reinforce for us to feel good about ourself or the relationship. In such instances, we clutch at anything that seems appealing, anything that makes us 'feel happy' (like attention without a purpose), until it loses its attraction, which tends to be pretty soon afterwards!

For example, most people would agree that being compatible with someone is the foundation for a marriage or a long-term friendship. Unfortunately, very few people make compatibility their priority during dating. Instead, they are driven to seek intimate contact on the basis of purely physical attraction and humour, instead of using those obvious elements as merely the starting point to establishing real compatibility. The whole package of attributes (physical, intellectual, emotional, warmth, values, expectations, self-confidence, aspirations, etc.) is what dictates mutual alignment and longevity in any relationship. Nothing else.

## The Power of Self-Knowledge

The reason so many people do not know what they want for their personal happiness is because they lack awareness of their own basic

*10 Easy Steps To....*

temperament, values and essential emotional needs. Self-knowledge is the most powerful advantage we have in living a good life and achieving our purpose. Yet many fear self-analysis or exploration, often living in denial of their own needs, unable to face themselves and their desires. Perhaps because they view themselves negatively in the belief that they do not deserve happiness and love, they fear any kind of critical exposure, remaining blissfully closed to their needs.

Most importantly, many are so used to accepting dull discomfort as their lot in life, being too fearful to experiment or to try something new, they probably wouldn't recognise happiness if it got up and smacked them in the face! Result: some people know what they are attracted to, but even fewer people know why, or how it relates to their innermost desires and needs for fulfilment. Instead they depend on others to 'supply' the happiness they seek and live in constant fear of losing it, which tends to make the relationship unfulfilling, short-term and heavily one-sided.

Not being sure of what makes us happy, the qualities we seek in others become clues in our search for personal reward – a key factor in attraction. There are many ways we might be rewarded, or be rewarding to others. Research shows that the most crucial of all is seeking others to confirm our persona and beliefs, thus increasing our feelings of significance and value (through affirmation and reinforcement).

Quite simply, once we are drawn to someone physically, **the secret and essence of any genuine attraction is mutual validation**. We enjoy the feeling of having our beliefs supported, our existence and aspirations confirmed and our fears allayed, so we band together with those who will oblige, and try to impress them, and easily exclude those who won't. This is part of the economics of attraction, which is discussed in the more detailed chapter on attraction in *Money, Sex and Compromise*, from which some of this key step is taken.


## The Search for Excitement

There are also different forms of attraction depending upon the age group of the individuals concerned. For example, young people

*10 Easy Steps To....*

have to experiment to learn and are likely to require a different set of qualities in a soulmate from the older folks around them: ones that relate to the need to belong, to be appreciated and wanted, to get attention and, above all, to be listened to. This is particularly true if these young people had parents who tended toward tighter discipline rather than praising, affirming or listening to them.

Parents' choice of partners for their children is usually based on intellectual and material needs, formed from their own knowledge and experience, while the youngsters themselves seek partners to satisfy physical, emotional and sexual needs. However, as a rule, the happier the life at home for the youngster, and the more she/he identifies with his/her parents, the more the choice of partner will converge with parental expectations.

The final element young people seek is excitement. And they get that in the early days of feeling 'in love' and besotted. In the absence of experience and knowledge, young adults have to rely upon their own instincts, physical demands and individual sensitivity to decide upon a mate. Thus they tend to go for the first few partners who appear to reduce their emotional costs and increase their happiness benefits, until experience and maturity alter their aspirations.

Attraction for most in-love couples at a youthful stage is thus spontaneous and more physical, giving maximum excitement – almost reckless, in fact. Ruled totally by emotion and physical needs, the young person has little time for the studied, logical advice of a parent, especially if this advice contradicts their own feelings!

So, with attraction being unpredictable and undisciplined, chance meetings often become serious relationships while, in contrast, the most deliberate efforts to engineer a love match between two people can often be fruitless, undone by sheer bad luck, bad timing or bad vibes. Indeed, something about your situation can make some people seem attractive to you one moment, and repellent to you in another place, or at another time. Hence the popularity and short life of holiday romances, which are dictated mainly by their context.

Notwithstanding all of that, what is at the root of the attraction process?

## The PIE Attraction Triangle

When attraction works we often say that the couple is experiencing great 'chemistry', and we are usually referring, mostly, to the physical aspects of attraction. Looks and body shape tend to become the key barometers. But, as important as physical attraction certainly is in drawing potential mates together, finding that crucial chemistry is seldom based solely upon appearance. Being changeable, highly superficial and dictated by the ageing process, appearance is a poor stabilising force in keeping partners bonded together.

That is why some people move from one 'trophy' partner to another. All they see is the outward appearance – the physical beauty – but not the limited intelligence, the lack of reinforcement or the emotional hang-ups, which soon reveal themselves in all their glory! An absence of the key qualities of attraction might be fine in the short-term but usually spells disaster in the long-term for any relationship. To find the basis of genuine attraction, one has to look at what is operating between two people on any given day; what I would call the PIE magnetic factors – a combination of **p**hysical, **i**ntellectual and **e**motional elements that influence every contact.

The greater the force of the PIE factors in the social intercourse with someone, the more we will want to align with them because we will be rewarded, affirmed and valued. If the PIE 'triangle' is weak, the interaction is unlikely to turn into a friendship and will always remain on a platonic, business or 'needs must' basis. Each element in this attraction triangle will also vary in importance depending upon our age or the stage we have reached in our life.

For example, the physical aspect of the triangle tends to dominate when we are younger and the intellectual when we are middle-aged and seeking stimulation as we explore the meaning of our life. The emotional aspect gathers momentum when we are older and need the warmth, affirmation and support of loved ones around us, or a special person with which to bond. At this older stage of life, the physical side of the triangle often has less importance.

As a result, any couple has to bond physically, intellectually and emotionally before they can

116

experience that essential 'chemistry' everyone desires, one that emphasises similarity in approach, a congruence of perspectives and reciprocity of purpose and values. Throw in some warmth and humour, and you have the ideal attraction base.

The longest relationships are based on having the most powerful combination of these PIE factors. On the other hand, where more than one PIE element is absent, surely, that's a brief relationship in the making!

## The PHYSICAL Factor

This is a key element in the attraction triangle, especially for females. Ours being a society fixated on appearance, physical attractiveness is a moderately good predictor of how often a female dates because men value this kind of attractiveness more than women. Not surprisingly, 90 per cent of cosmetic surgery patients are women! Physical attractiveness not only helps to create a positive first impression, it is also associated with fertility and health – in other words, the selection of the best people to ensure ongoing reproduction of our species.

However, physical attraction is not just about looks, body form, shape, hair and eyes. It also incorporates material things (such as money, possessions, status, success), the lifestyle enjoyed and the level of personal creativity. These all combine to create the perfect, attractive physical package.

This part of the attraction process is very powerful because no matter how we might search for the 'inner beauty' of a person, we are drawn to their outer looks first! That is Nature's deliberate way of getting us together. That is all we can see before establishing anything else about that person. So, don't believe anyone who says they 'don't care about looks but what's inside'. That's pie in the sky!

In that case, they might as well go with a chimp or a horse because it is what's inside that matters! We cannot see anyone's 'inside' before we see their physicality! That comes later. The reason why anyone might profess that is perhaps due to their low self-esteem (shyness or non-affirmation). They do not value their own looks or self, and so they devalue others too, while hoping that no one will notice their looks

118

either. Anyway, what keeps us apart from our ideal in a partner is the personal identikit we have put together and carry around in our head based upon a mental image of what the 'perfect soulmate' should be like.

When we see someone with the physical characteristics which match such so-called ideals as being 'tall, dark, and handsome', 'a Diana Ross or Madonna clone', 'a blonde bombshell', or a 'Denzel Washington or Brad Pitt lookalike', we get very excited. Something in our psyche makes us immediately think, 'This is *the one!*'

However, if we rely strictly upon these narrow definitions of what is attractive, we are likely to miss other people, for example those across age, class or cultural lines, who do not entirely fit our imprinted image of the perfect partner, but who may come closer to the ideal than is immediately apparent.

We often hear the cliché that 'opposites attract', but they don't, in fact. No research has reliably shown that opposites really attract. Instead, most surveys have shown that people like best those who are most like themselves!

Certain obvious elements like skin colour and religion might differ, but partners who are significantly opposed in belief, perception and behaviour would find little point of contact or agreement, which would make for a frustrating, stressful and insecure situation.

Similarity in beliefs, values, perception, behaviour and type appears to be the key to mutual attraction. The reason why shared interests and similarity are so important is because of a basic need for reciprocity (mutual giving and reinforcement) and for being accepted as we wish to be. Put simply, **we like those who like and affirm us**.

Anyone showing that they prefer us tends to make us respond in kind. Where there is little reciprocity, it affects self-esteem because it removes the reason to be proud and the sense of achievement in one's activities. It also negates the values one cherish and denies the feeling of significance and value.

✳ ✳ ✳ ✳ ✳ ✳

*For every minute you are angry, you lose sixty seconds of happiness.*

Ralph Waldo Emerson

*10 Easy Steps To....*

## The INTELLECTUAL Factor

When there is a willingness to be challenged intellectually, to engage in stimulating conversation and to drool over what we like, there is often an enjoyable meeting of minds that can help any relationship to take root. Being intellectually compatible does not mean a high level of college-based education on both sides. It can relate to simple common sense and intelligence, having experience of other cultures and peoples or being knowledgeable in a specific field. Intellectual attraction reveals itself in personal interests, cherished values and preferred life purpose.

An individual may find a strong attraction to another person because they both share a similar purpose (e.g. protecting the environment, fighting for justice, walking for fundraising, etc.) or through a mutual interest. They may both love the same sports team, enjoy dancing, going for cycle rides, visiting an art museum, or playing a good game of Scrabble, for example. Whatever the common link, even if it is just discussing hobbies, music or football teams, it could prove to be the intellectual glue that will keep their relationship together.

The main aspect of being intellectually appealing is to have interactions that both parties enjoy and which confirm and reinforce our experience. For example, a university boffin might find someone very attractive physically. But if there is little experience of life to hold a conversation over the candle-lit dinner there will be no mutual points to share, which makes a repeat outing highly unlikely!

The best way to be intellectually appealing is to read a lot, take an interest in your world and others, join activity clubs, keep up with current affairs and have some opinions on them, develop hobbies, self-educate, keep abreast of technology or acquire formal qualifications. All of these help to broaden your outlook, increase your knowledge and expertise and it keep you on par with your mate. The most appealing person is one who knows his/her limits and is not afraid to ask for information, explanation or clarification. In short, to continually self-educate.

Conversely, someone who appears to know everything, or is always finding fault in order to demonstrate their knowledge and superiority, will most certainly be avoided because they are

122

not positive or affirming, being only interested in themselves and proving how right they are. Even if you are more intellectually adept than your partner, being slow to dominate every conversation with your opinions allows the other person to contribute to the interaction in a more meaningful way for them.

The strongest tip for an intellectual match on a new date is that the biggest sexual organ is your brain. Therefore, if you are not seduced on your own intellectual level before the emotional part kicks in, don't go there. If it doesn't feel right in conversation or on the phone, don't go there. If there are long and embarrassing pauses, or the person is not really interested in what you are saying and feeling, please don't go there. Otherwise, that is likely to be a very flat connection without much substance to hold it together!

**The EMOTIONAL Factor**

This important human aspect involves openness, honesty, caring, warmth, being mutually attentive, committed and vulnerable to some degree. We all crave love with romance and passion, in particular, but many are not prepared to surrender personal control or to feel vulnerable to get it.

My colleague Phil claims to have many friends rather than lovers, because he does not wish to leave himself open to be hurt. Instead he takes refuge in his work and numerous activities while making excuses for his fear and lack of commitment. This is a real pity because he is very attractive, warm, successful and rich – a most eligible bachelor by any standards!

Many people like Phil tend to forget that pleasure usually comes before hurt while any hurt we experience strengthens our ability to deal with future relationships. It is also about taking risks. If we don't take any risks, especially after we have been hurt, we miss out on any future pleasure and pain, remaining emotionally constipated in fearful angst. By deliberately avoiding any hurt, we also lose out on the experience of dealing with intimate interactions and learning from them. We keep repeating the same mistakes, lacking the full range of emotions that, in turn, make us more appealing. We are then left with those fearful attitudes and behaviours which take no effort to maintain but which, gradually, rob us of a life.

At the core of our emotional make-up is self-awareness: how we manage our emotions, whether we are calm and collected or we panic quickly, our level of compassion and empathy towards others, and the level of humour, talent and depth we each possess; whether we take ourselves too seriously or we lack substance. These are all part of our emotional appeal.

For example, look at any lonely heart advertisement and the key word in it will be the need to find someone with 'GSOH' (good sense of humour). The easiest form of attraction is thus for someone to make us laugh, one who has a fun personality to enhance our own. But it has to be reciprocal to actually work.

## The Search For Upliftment

There are many grumpy, gloomy pessimists who believe that simply finding someone with a good sense of humour will make them happier. But happiness and good humour are created inside of us first. People who actively seek happiness, who seek humour or seek other things they lack, tend to be hard work themselves! They are likely to emphasise what they want from a partner rather than what they have to give too which robs the connection of its reciprocity.

Most important, happiness and a sense of humour are not end goals we strive towards. They are interactive states of being that we can develop and use to good effect every single day. Thus finding someone with a good sense of humour is desirable, but it works only if you can appreciate the humour too, or are already sufficiently happy to align with that humour. When we are too selfish to give, too busy to appreciate others, too reluctant to open ourselves to loved ones or we feel inadequate in ourselves, we then look for people to *make* us happy – to provide that essential spark to bring us to life.

But other people merely enhance, or reduce, your happiness, they do not create or generate it. Thus a new soulmate might momentarily enhance your pleasurable feelings, but those feelings cannot be maintained without self-acceptance and self-love, the twin foundations of personal happiness. If you have no happiness inside you in the first place, your partner's consistent extroversion and positive outlook will gradually irritate you, making you feel resentful when the novelty begins to wear off. You will also feel even worse when the relationship ends.

## Passionate Love

What we most crave – passionate love, with all the fireworks attached – is usually a state of intense longing for union with another person with whom we share strong chemistry. Passionate lovers are absorbed in one another, feel ecstatic at gaining their partner's love and are distressed upon losing it. They share intense emotional bonding and disclosure. Thus it is difficult to sustain passion when one is not emotionally, and verbally, prepared to do so. Self-disclosure and openness encourage the deepest emotional bonding and passion, but many people fear disclosure of any kind, if it reveals too much of themselves. They often remain in a kind of superficial limbo that deprives them of truly passionate relationships.

For example, I am an open person who feels secure in myself and tend to trust others, until they prove otherwise. I love to talk with others, to hear their opinions on things that affect them. Nothing is taboo to further the process of learning and self-development. This was also matched to a great extent by David's personality. However, I discovered that when my marriage began to deteriorate, my partner and I increasingly had more no-go areas in discussion topics than it was possible to imagine.

We were so afraid of saying the 'wrong' thing that we stopped talking altogether, except for the bare essentials; stopped sharing and stopped reciprocating. We simply argued without listening, expecting each other to capitulate in favour of individual egos. Fear of criticism and accusation dominated every interaction. What a joy it was later on to communicate with my new soulmate on any subject; to discuss topics, actions, intentions and anxieties without fear, blame or favour. It was an incredibly liberating experience.

The basis of attraction between two people is mutual stimulation on physical, intellectual and emotional levels. Having two out of three factors might keep the relationship going for a while, but one out of three hasn't a hope in hell of lasting, unless the other person is similarly endowed! The contrast between what is available at home and what is possible outside with someone else would eventually prove too great to resist.

~~~~~~~~~~~~~~~~~~~~~~~~~~~~~~~~~~~~

## *Exercise Four*

How close do you feel to your current date or spouse on a routine basis? Find out with the questions below:

A. Do you feel ecstatic? Excited? Or just luke-warm in the other person's presence?

B. Do you want to touch them a lot and do you find it hard to keep your eyes off them? Or does the remoteness in your body language speak volumes?

C. Rate your feelings out of 10. If the result is under five, then the relationship needs urgent attention. If you are still at the dating stage and have such a low score, this relationship is not likely to be going very far!

D. How long have you felt this way?

E. Would you say that the chemistry between you has changed dramatically since you first *met, or has it tended to be like it is now?*

Your emotions are the clearest guide to how you feel and what makes you happy. If you ignore them you ignore your desires, your growth and your happiness. You are likely to exist in persistent frustration and anxiety without really understanding or knowing why.

~~~~~~~~~~~~~~~~~~~~~~~~~~~~~~~~~~~

**REFLECTION**

Step Four in *Finding Your Ideal Soulmate....*

## *MAKE SURE YOU HAVE CHEMISTRY!*

... This not only helps the relationship to last longer, it also adds the kind of excitement that many people are seeking when they fall in love.

✳ ✳ ✳ ✳ ✳ ✳

*The choice between love and fear is made every moment in our hearts and minds. That is where the peace process begins. Without peace within, peace in the world is an empty wish.*
*Like love, peace is extended.*

Paul Ferrini

# ~ STEP FIVE ~

## Communication

According to Mintel[4], over six million people in the U.K now seek partners on the Internet compared to a quarter of a million who do so through introduction agencies. Thanks to Internet dating, people don't even have to leave their homes at all to seek a soulmate. In complete privacy and convenience, and at the press of a button, they can either allow or deny access to their company. Women, especially, have benefited from this safer, more confident, form of dating. However, this way of seeking a partner is still in its relative infancy and is surrounded by a lot of superstition, suspicion, anxiety and expectations, especially from people who don't really understand its benefits, how to use it effectively or how it actually works. Most important, it means the rules are changing for interacting with any potential mate.

In pre-Internet days one would first meet someone face-to-face and then begin the slow task of getting to know that person through conversation, activities and focus – mainly trial and error! Now it is the exact opposite. People converse first, both online and on the telephone, and then meet. By the time they do face each other, each will have learned a lot about the other person, but only in the abstract.

That first face-to-face meeting often brings its own anxieties because no one is ever really prepared for it. Additionally, because some people do lie about themselves, there is always the fear that the one-dimensional conversation and picture won't match up with the three-dimensional person. So there is a lot of fretting and soul-searching beforehand until that important meeting dispels all doubt.

All this makes communication within the dating process extremely important because we don't only communicate with words, we also speak with every part of us: through our mood, body language and actual behaviour.

## We Always Send out a Message

Communication is the key to aligning with another human being and yet many people either fear communication, ignore it, abuse it or deny it. We are ALWAYS communicating through silent messages, no matter what we do, and especially when we are not saying a word. The way we sit, stare, go quiet, laugh, frown, fold our arms, raise our eyebrows or respond wordlessly to a comment, are all dead giveaways as to how we feel in the presence of another.

For example, if you try to hold someone and they back off that is a sure sign that the chemistry is not really there and they do not feel the way you do about the situation. If the person's responses are also lukewarm and distant, you are wasting your time and efforts, or you are moving in too soon.

Perhaps because I like connecting with people on different levels, I am very sensitive to various forms of communication. I am careful to avoid the most awesomely self-centred people, to avoid misinterpreting their reaction or

134

engaging someone who really isn't interested in me. Yet a lack of connection (through boredom, disappointment or rejection) can be avoided in communication by some simple helpful hints.

We communicate for specific purposes, no matter the generalised message our body is giving. If we meet someone we do not like, unconsciously our barriers go up to protect us from any further encroachment by that person. We go into 'flight' mode, while we pretend as much as possible that we are in 'engaged' mode. Yet all we want to do is to leave that situation. Some people have the courage to do just that by finding plausible excuses, while others say nothing and let their body speak instead. Interestingly, the more we pretend to like a negative situation the more our body and actions quietly show their disapproval!

So it is not worth prolonging an unwanted interaction because no one is done any favours by it. On the other hand, when we meet those we like, all we want to do is to reach out and touch them, to have a rapport with them by mirroring their stance and words and to be reflected by them. Those are all different forms of communicating how we feel, and the presence or absence of such alignment or 'chemistry' dictates the content and tone of that communication.

In negative situations, it is always best to clearly say that you don't feel any chemistry and curtail the interaction, unless there are other reasons to continue, like wanting basic friendship instead. But it has to be mutual. Mind you, one has to be careful too about writing off someone in the first few minutes of a meeting, because that is what I did with David!

I didn't warm to him much when I first saw him and wasted no time in telling him so! Luckily, he liked me and had the confidence and presence of mind to offer me lunch, which allowed his personality to gradually emerge. The rest is history. If he had been thin-skinned and had judged me as quickly as I did him, I would have missed the time of my life!

## Cultivating Inclusive Dialogue

Communication of all kinds is crucial when seeking a soulmate because it is like putting our assets on display to attract a buyer. A weak display appears ambiguous and is likely to repel buyers, or even attract the wrong ones – those who want to devalue our goods. A strong display should attract only those genuinely interested, which immediately reduces the field only to those worth considering.

Communication is thus a form of interest, first and foremost. If the verbal part of that communication does not reflect and/or justify the initial interest, very little will develop afterwards. Interest then shows itself in dialogue. But this is often where problems begin because many people do not understand what dialogue is all about.

A dialogue is not just two people trying to make small talk by conversing. Rather, it is an important communication tool which, when used adeptly, should answer all sorts of questions about the other person, topic, or situation, while moving the budding friendship along at a healthy pace. Conversations can be very revealing of the speakers if we really focus upon what is being said. But often we are not really interested in that person. So, instead of using conversation to enhance our interest, it is used to actually create interest!

In such cases questions are asked without any purpose, or not asked at all. Only statements are made, which does little to help general understanding. That is why many potential friendships fail to flower because, in these situations, it is like putting the cart before the horse!

James will never forget this girl who called him, apparently to get to know him, and then kept talking incessantly. She would ask him a question and then, even before he began to answer it, she would jump in to tell him something else about herself. He wondered why she bothered to ask him anything! All she wanted to talk about was how she loved to dress up, how she liked her men to dress up too, how she appreciated the good things of life, how she kept herself fit for her age, etc. – over and over again. Nothing was wrong with that, if it was taken in perspective and suited the context, but she really wasn't interested in James at all. This wasn't a dialogue about them both, only a smooth presentation about herself.

While James listened intently and wanted to get to know her through her answers, showing due respect for her as an individual, she was not

*10 Easy Steps To....*

listening to him at all because that was not her agenda. She merely wanted an audience. She was just waiting for him to shut up, never allowing him to finish his sentences, so that she could continue admiring herself!

The real tragedy for James was that she sounded very affable and friendly, but he said that he immediately imagined himself on a date with her and recoiled at what he would have had to endure. He quickly found an excuse to send her on her way.

If we genuinely wish to get to know someone, the dialogue we have with him/her should reflect that. It should allow ample opportunity for both requesting and offering information. Above all, it should contain three key elements, in this order:

A. Interest in the person and their activities

B. Questions that reflect such interest

C. Affirmation and reinforcement of the other party

Once I befriended a rather introspective woman for about two months and in all that time she never once asked me how I was! Yet she said I was such a friend to her. She asked me nothing relating to my life, to my joys or pain, to my feelings or aspirations, or any part of my day. It was as though I was some sort of invisible, unfeeling oracle she consulted and talked to about her current troubles.

Her introspection was so stark, I was quite fascinated by how one person could be so wrapped up in herself and yet still expect to connect with other human beings successfully! But, of course, that could be why she was having interaction problems with others.


## The Value of Personal Interest

Any relationship is less about you, and more about the potential soulmate. If that person remembers the same thing too, then you both have the ideal start to explore possibilities – simple mutual interest.

Showing interest is the most basic beginning and it must be genuine, whether you are talking to that person online, on the phone or face-to-face. You really must find the other person interesting, otherwise you are unlikely to enjoy the connection and might come to resent the time spent on it. You will feel bored and distracted and the person can easily feel rejected, even if this is not your intention or desire.

The basis of communication is finding out what type of person you are dealing with, and whether they are worthy of your interest and will relate to you in any way. This should be revealed in what they stand for (**values**), what they want in their life (**desires**), where they are going (**aspirations**) and what they hope for in a soulmate (**expectations**). These four things are crucial to the development of the friendship.

Once the simple contact questions about name, personal details and occupation are out of the way, other exploratory questions should be framed in a subtle way around those four areas to get a greater measure of the person. Soon you will start hearing things that will either attract or repel, but which will help you to decide where you wish to go with that person.

Interest is shown through the questions you ask. If you ask no questions, you will get few answers. Sooner rather than later, the conversation will come to a dead stop because one party will run out of questions, or might even resent not being asked any in order to reveal themselves. Here are two examples of getting-to-know-you online dialogues.

The first one consists of responses (merely statements) that clearly exclude the questioner, giving her little chance of contributing, while the second allows both parties to feel included. By the way, 'lol' means 'laugh out loud':

| | |
|---|---|
| Mexican49: | Like your profile! |
| Execbag: | You do? Thanks...and who am I speaking to? |
| Mexican49: | Martin |
| Execbag: | Tanya...pleased to meet you. Where in Berks? |
| Mexican49: | Sunningdale |
| Execbag: | Oh, the posh part...I am slumming in Reading...lol |
| Mexican49: | sure you're not slumming |
| Execbag: | Oh yes, I have my little knapsack at the ready each day! |
| Mexican49: | An executive person like you? |
| Execbag: | Mmmmm...one has to keep up one's appearances, even with knapsack. |
| Mexican49: | sure you do!, Harrods knapsack, I bet! |
| Execbag: | Lol..love it! So what exciting things |

142

|            | have you planned for the weekend? |
|------------|-----------------------------------|
| Mexican49: | not sure yet, may wander down to the coast |
| Execbag:   | Do you do that often? |
| Mexican49: | yes |
| Execbag:   | Surely, you don't sea bathe at this time of year? |
| Mexican49: | no! |
| Mexican49: | I like the restaurants though and to watch people bathe |
| Execbag:   | So why the coast? For fresh air? For mermaids?...lol |
| Mexican49: | mermaids, yes |
| Execbag:   | Ahhhh...I seee..lol |
| Execbag:   | What other things do you like doing? |
| Mexican49: | cooking, travel, having fun |
| Execbag:   | So what are you seeking on here? |
| Mexican49: | not on here much, actually |
| Mexican49: | but nice to meet sensible fun people |
| Execbag:   | So why today? |
| Mexican49: | had some time this morning |
| Execbag:   | I see...that's good. Helps relaxation, I suppose. |

Finding Your Ideal Soulmate!

| Mexican49: | yes it does |
| Mexican49: | Not on here with any agenda, just a fun single guy |
| Execbag: | Okay |
| Mexican49: | like relaxing with good company |
| Execbag: | Right |

## The Power of Questions

Only one person asked the questions in that dialogue, which lasted about 10 minutes. The other person was not really drawn into reveal ing anything about herself. While she is learning about him and his activities, he is learning nothing about her. Not surprisingly, after a while, she loses interest in finding out any more about him or in asking any further questions. The conversation thus peters out to just the simple 'Okay' and 'Right' at the end. Nothing much would follow from that if there were no questions from him. Contrast it to the dialogue below:

| Mexican49: | Like your profile! |
| Execbag: | You do? Thanks...And who am I speaking to? |

| | |
|---|---|
| Mexican49: | Martin |
| Execbag: | Tanya...pleased to meet you. Where in Berks? |
| Mexican49: | Sunningdale |
| Execbag: | Oh, the posh part...I am slumming in Reading...lol |
| Execbag: | I have my little knapsack at the ready each day! |
| Mexican49: | an executive person like you? |
| Mexican49: | I'm sure you're not...so what's your interests? |
| Execbag: | Varied..but walking, reading, music, dancing and theatre would come right to the top. |
| Mexican49: | very much the same for me |
| Execbag: | Do you dance a lot? |
| Mexican49: | no, but I like theatre, food and wine |
| Mexican49: | and of course travel |
| Execbag: | I dance quite a bit...I go to salsa on Thursdays and disco on Saturdays and walking on Sundays. I do love all types of music which stirs me. |
| Mexican49: | I like a wide range of music myself |
| Execbag: | I like travelling too but, as I don't get an opportunity to leave my business, I can only go at certain times. |

| Mexican49: | what business are you in? |
| Execbag: | Advertising and promotion..but I am still learning. What about you? |
| Execbag: | I am in IT programming as a consultant. |
| Mexican49: | I spend a lot of time in Hungary at the moment |
| Execbag: | Why is that? |
| Mexican49: | I have some business there and I like the place and people |
| Mexican49: | what do you like about your job? |
| Execbag: | All kinds of things actually, but I guess I love the product promotion. Seeing people being influenced by what we create. |
| Execbag: | Have you been consulting for long? |
| Mexican49: | yes , 7 yrs now. |
| Execbag: | We have been going for 2 years and I really enjoy it, especially working for myself. |
| Mexican49: | Where do you want the business to go? |
| Execbag: | Obviously as successful as possible... lol! |

In this conversation, the balance of the dialogue is much more even. As a result, both speakers are revealing a lot about themselves through their answers. The conversation flows from one topic to the other without awkward pauses or single link words. Each is keen to reveal their activities and aspirations and, as they both have the chance to do so, they appear more interesting to, and interested in, each other.

A dialogue is like a tennis game. If you hold on to the ball (always talking or remaining silent) there is no game and the other party will easily feel bored or awkward. Thus statements have to go hand-in-hand with questions. Anyone who never asks questions needs to develop their interactive skills because the essence of any good dialogue is not responses but the questions asked, which can be both initiated and returned by either party.

No one can feel included or appealing if the other person seems uninterested in her/him. Furthermore, once that person has gone on and on for a while without pausing to let you in, they cease to be of any real interest. All you want is for them to just shut up! End of potential friendship before it even began.

People who are insecure, unduly nervous, arrogant, overbearing, unskilled socially and self-absorbed always tend to talk endlessly about themselves and their 'exciting' activities without letting in the other person at all. They believe that what they are doing is so unique, extraordinary or wonderful it deserves constant airing to the exclusion of all else! Result: a continuing monologue involving only one person instead of a genuine dialogue between two individuals. Even worse, such people may never change since they are unlikely to get the chance to develop their listening skills, and listening is the most important part of any successful conversation.

## Affirmation and Reinforcement

Had the last conversation carried on much longer, there would have been examples of affirmation and reinforcement emerging – a natural process when two people are interested in one another, are enjoying the connection and wish to impress each other. Any good dialogue must contain these twin elements in order to move the friendship forward. The focus is on what the other party is saying and also on mirroring their conversation by selecting key excerpts to comment upon, to affirm or to reinforce. This shows both alignment with the speaker and an appreciation of their life. For example, the following brief banter reflects this further:

| | |
|---|---|
| Mexican49: | so what have you been doing today? |
| Execbag: | Preparing for my forthcoming athletic event in Munich |
| Mexican49: | you've been to Munich? I have too...what do you think of it? |
| Execbag: | It's wonderful... did you enjoy it? |
| Mexican49: | yep, especially the first time I went there and tried their beers....but am more interested in you being an athlete? you must find it hard work... |
| Execbag: | Oh yes, I do, but it has its rewards. I have won a few medals. |
| Mexican49: | a few medals!! tell me more.. you must be very clever. |
| Execbag: | I am sure you are clever too, being a consultant. You must be an expert to be at that level. lol |
| Mexican49: | oh, I try my best, but I bet you put in a lot of training.... wow! I am talking |

to a famous athlete! lol

Execbag: Don't make it sound like that.....
Nothing more than your
achievements...lol

Notice that there is mutual admiration, affirmation and reinforcement as both show genuine
interest in the other and mirror key words like
'Munich', 'athlete', 'medals' and 'consultant'.
When we do not mirror any words in our
responses it means we are hardly listening to the
other party, which results in little reinforcement
or expansion of what they hold dear and care
about. To affirm and reinforce someone shows
value and appreciation for who they are and a
generosity of spirit in acknowledging them on
their terms.

With online dialogue, you can also pick up a
lot of clues to people's personalities, like the fact
that Mexican49 seems far less formal and
'correct' in his manner and use of words than
Execbag, who uses clear sentences. This is significant because it is likely that she will be more
formal too in other aspects! If his approach is
too blasé, he might begin to irritate her later on
or he might think she's too 'stuffy'.

## Avoiding Conflicting Signals

Affirmation and reinforcement are positive actions that emphasise what the person means to us. If your date or spouse is embarrassed by affirmation, praise and reinforcement, it is a sign that they feel they do not deserve it, or that you do not deserve it either! If you admired someone's photo, for example, and you tell them how good they looked but they say nothing about your photo too, that is a huge warning sign of what's to come. They are obviously not used to affirming and reinforcing others, perhaps because they are not usually affirmed themselves or are deliberately withholding such affirmation to be controlling. These seemingly trivial instances reveal a lot and it won't get any better.

Nadia was the recipient of this treatment by a man who kept telling her that she was 'fishing for compliments' whenever she genuinely showed appreciation for him by praising him in any way. Yet this man was also receiving attention from two other women simultaneously, each of whom he was controlling and stringing along to boost his own ego, neither of whom he attempted to affirm or reinforce by complimenting them. He didn't have to 'fish for compliments'. He just made sure he got them through the ultimate compliment – someone else's attention, regardless of their needs or the ethics involved!

Communicating clearly in words about ourselves, our desires and what we seek in a partnership will save conflicting body language later on. Returning the 'ball' in our dialogue ensures that one individual does not hog the conversation. Instead, it is evenly balanced and each person feels valued and included by both contributing and being heard. It also allows for a more interesting conversation and a positive development of the friendship, while providing some information for the parties to make the right choices about each other.

Not only that, people will love to converse with you because they will not only enjoy the interaction, but you will also appear even more appealing due to that interest and reinforcement.

~~~~~~~~~~~~~~~~~~~~~~~~~~~~~~~~~~~~

### *Exercise Five*

How do you talk to potential dates at the moment? Is it all about you or them? Do you ask any questions? Or are you usually left out of the dialogue because the other person talked too much and you were too shy to assert yourself? Do you actually listen to the other person or are you too busy thinking about the next thing you wish to say? Try this exercise and see:

A. *Consider carefully the conversations that took place on the last two dates you had (or in your relationship) and try to work out the stage at which they stopped in their tracks. What really caused the breakdowns?*

B. *Were the conversations inclusive or exclusive? Interesting or bland? Defensive or supportive?*

C. *What didn't you genuinely like about the connections you were making with significant others in your life? (It could also be a question of clashing values.)*

D. *How could you have made a difference to those situations, or even to the present ones?*

Finding Your Ideal Soulmate!

By identifying what you really did not like every time a date (or conversation) did not produce the desired result, you will be able to see whether it was the dialogue, the information being revealed, or withheld, the expectations or the actions involved which were the culprits. Being competent at conversing will not only take the friendship further, it will also leave you with one thing less to worry about when you are trying to impress someone new! If you are in a relationship already, good communication should bond you closer and help to resolve any issues, as long as both parties are also willing to listen and to allow expression of basic feelings.

~~~~~~~~~~~~~~~~~~~~~~~~~~~~~~~~~

## REFLECTION

Step Five in *Finding Your Ideal Soulmate*....

## KNOW HOW TO COMMUNICATE!

.... Clear communication that says what you mean, and which involves and affirms others, is a sure winner every time. It provides the necessary information needed for both parties to either make progress or beat a hasty retreat!

*10 Easy Steps To....*

# ~ STEP SIX ~

## Expectation

So you see the man or woman you fancy across the room at a party. You edge nervously towards him/her, wanting to make that crucial impression. You finally make the connection between you and you feel really happy. You punch the air with joy. A few weeks – or even years – later, everything stops in its tracks and you can't understand it. End of beautiful romance or marriage. And what killed it, you wonder? Ah, those *expectations*. They just did not match up between you.

Expectations are the biggest killers of all relationships, whether new or established, since unrealistic demands and the search for perfection invariably suck the lifeblood out of a connection. Every partnership that breaks down begin its downfall when expectations go unfulfilled, which then causes frustration, resentment, anger and even violence. High expectations and the desire for perfection in our soulmates gradually erode the love and good feelings we initially have. Disappointment creeps in, a re-evaluation takes place that pushes our feelings for our partners toward the negative, and respect is gradually lost.

There are two main kinds of expectations: those that seek to change our soulmates into some perfect ideal of the desired person, and those that are impossible to fulfil because they go against our basic values and purpose. They rob of us our freedom, free choice and unique perspectives. Worst of all, they make us feel inadequate and forever below par. Both kinds of expectations are so unrealistic they are hardly ever achieved, and yet people continue to strive in vain, every day, to realise them. Wherever such expectations are fulfilled, there is likely to be a significant element of controlling, browbeating and even bullying.

There is also the anxious kind of expectation which fears commitment and assumes either that everyone is out to trap us into a long-term relationship, or that they should already have been partnering us!

## Gender Conflict in Expectations

There is a saying that men marry women hoping they will stay the same forever while women marry men hoping to change them as soon as the ceremony is over! Expectations that involve seeking perfection are particularly soul destroying. The main trouble with wanting perfection in a relationship is that one partner's idea of perfection will rarely coincide with that of the other, and so the desire to compete for this elusive state inevitably gets out of hand as the resulting expectations gradually damage the relationship. One can see this perfect ideal long before the two people have settled into the relationship – at the dating stage, in fact.

It rears its ugly head whenever individuals express the desire not to connect with anyone

158

with emotional or other 'baggage'. They want a perfect being without negative feelings – perhaps without any feelings at all, so long as they are 'happy'! But this so-called 'baggage' contains our pain, hurt and essential issues to be resolved. It also contains our resources from which we can learn to rebuild our lives. It is an inevitable process that is crucial to our development and forms the core of who we are. The ideal situation is to carry this 'baggage' in reducing amounts until we learn from it and let it go. But many people pretend they have no baggage at all. They mask it with a lot of 'fun', 'humour' or unforgiving seriousness while they die inside, becoming unfeeling and insensitive robots.

Every part of our experience becomes a kind of baggage that shapes our perception, alters our attitudes and is then put aside in our ongoing development.

As I said in my other book on relationships, "To meet someone claiming to be without any baggage is to meet a bland, fearful idiot, unable to cope with his/her emotions or feelings; someone pretending about their life; who is constantly in denial that nothing affects them unduly, while denying others the right to their own emotions and feelings. However, it is not the 'baggage' we carry which is the main problem. It is how we handle that baggage, what we have in it, and how long we carry it for!" (Sihera - *Money, Sex & Compromise*[5])


## Conforming to Expectations

A desire for perfection means we are never happy with our partners or ourselves; never satisfied with our lives or our looks. There is always someone, or something, better waiting just around the corner. When we meet the desired one, they have to conform to our expectations by behaving in a prescribed manner in order to merit our attention and approval.

We are not prepared to let that person unfold gradually before us, to just be themselves and surprise us with something different, en route to what might turn out to be the same end. Instead, we have high expectations about how the partner should look (like the age-old cliché of 'looking sexy in a little black number') and how they should act in public ('mustn't drink beer from pint glasses' or 'must have the right designer car and clothes'), according to our perfect identikits.

What many people don't realise is that, should their soulmate change into the perfect ideal required, they both will soon be seeking different partners! Think about it carefully. People come together because they are attracted to each other – AS THEY ARE – not what they hope to be. Change one person to something else and she/he will then be looking for a new partner to match the new character-istics they have acquired.

That is why people who are promoted at work and those who undertake self-development or higher education courses during their relation-ships tend to gravitate towards those in a similar situation, if their spouses haven't kept up with them. Their new status would create new expectations.

Moreover, expectations and the search for perfection tend to blind us to the fact that we are far from perfect ourselves. There is a lot we too need to do to become 'perfect' in the eyes of others, like lose that 'beer belly', stop smoking, treat others more sensitively, become more caring, etc.. The end result is that we continually circle each other with high expectations, but with no capacity to fulfil them. At the same time we miss many opportunities for greater happiness just by being ourselves and enjoying it.

## Going Against Personal Belief

The second kind of expectations, those which challenge our values, can cause deep hurt and anxiety because they can be very difficult to fulfil, hitting at the heart of what we believe in and what gives us comfort and reinforcement. When we expect someone to do something that is against their basic beliefs, it can be increasingly stressful because they really do not want to do it. However, they might feel their partner's love is conditional upon its fulfilment and do it merely to please – not the best reason for taking action in such circumstances.

For example, it was not until John left his marriage that he realised how much financial security mattered to his wife, Karen. It didn't matter that much to him because he was a pioneer and security was always the last thing he would think of when challenging boundaries and breaking new ground. He gradually realised how his impulsiveness and lack of permanence would have really frightened her and how difficult it must have been for her to support his aims and objectives when they were so opposed to her own.

Yet he could not cease to be pioneering anymore than she could give up that desire for security and order in her environment. So his wife grew increasingly fearful while he also grew resentful. But John understood the way their different expectations and fears affected their behaviour only after they parted and he got some counselling. You might also expect that during the 18 years of their relationship Karen and John would have had the measure of each other at some point. But the fact that they didn't is not so strange.

People naturally evolve and the person you were at 21 will bear little relationship to the person emerging at 45. Not only will the ensuing years and experience change you dramatically but the impact of the relationship itself, in having to constantly accommodate another person in your life, also changes your outlook. As we get older, we tend to become more fearful of life and actually 'regress to type'. So what might have been a breeze for us when we were younger feels more problematic as we get older because we feel less resourceful and less equipped to deal with it. Our values are likely to have changed too and we might no longer wish to associate with that aspect of our past.

## When Expectations Clash

At the other end of the relationship scale, Gareth Sibson (author of *Single White Failure*[6]) gave a good example of how expectations can ruin something even before it begins. He took a 'nice girl' to dinner once. They had a great time and he thought he would think about the possibility of another date, though he was not sure he wanted to repeat it. A week went by and he did not contact her since he had still not made a decision. Imagine his surprise when she rang him to say how annoyed she was that he hadn't been in touch because when she was 'in a relationship' she expected to be treated differently.

This was news to him.

He perceived the meal as a 'getting-to-know-you' experience, one more educational and exploratory than decisive, whereas she enjoyed the date and perceived it to be the start of a relationship between them. His expectation was one of 'wait-and-see' while hers was one of him being already an item with her, a situation which carried certain rights and responsibilities with it. Quite different expectations being generated between two people who barely knew each other or their respective values.

It takes more than one date to establish a relationship, unless that date immediately leads to further intimate actions that clearly suggest deep liking, lust or even love. What makes expectations such a significant force is the way it dictates your attitude towards your partner and determines your treatment of him/her, while making you impotent in controlling their expectations of you.

True relationships come with alignment of thought, values, desires and purpose; with expectations that harmonise with one another and a real need to share time with that person, to give them attention and support. As expectations define the outcome of any relationship, so they need to be congruent between the two parties at the very beginning, and that is where good communication comes in.

## The True Power of Expectations

Expectations mainly reflect desires. When you live by yourself, you can fulfil your expectations easily as their gratification does not depend upon someone else. But in any relationship there is a mutual sharing of love and you cannot determine how your partner will share that love with you. Her or his expectations are always a mystery, yet it is the biggest decider of the direction the union will take. In living with a partner, you not only have *two* sets of expectations to take into account, you also have to contemplate how each of the reactions to those expectations will impact upon the relationship itself. This crucial four-way situation is illustrated with the following example.

If you expect your soulmate to take an afternoon off to support your activity, that is one expectation. However, she might expect you to

166                          *10 Easy Steps To....*

go ahead without her because she will be too busy. That's another expectation. Both are important to what actually happens on that particular afternoon. However, the key effect will depend on how you both feel about the expectation of each other. If you feel good about her lack of support, then that's a resolution. But if you both feel aggrieved because you believe the reaction to the 'reasonable' expectation is unreasonable, then that will have immediate repercussions. It will not only create disappointment and resentment, it will also have a negative impact on the activities that follow. So, as you can see, the power of expectations can affect our relationships without us even being aware of it.

As difficult as it might seem, expectations need to be realistic. They need to reflect what both parties would desire rather than just relating to one person. If your man decides to play golf every Friday and you would like to go somewhere else on a Friday, then a realistic expectation is to encourage him to give up some Friday golf in favour of your activity, while he continues with his hobby on the other days as usual. The answer is not to unrealistically expect him to give it all up for your desire. He might do that under pressure but it will eventually cause deep resentment. Additionally, if he refuses to budge in your favour, that shows a lack of respect for your needs, or a desire to dominate the partnership, which would need to be addressed.

Another example, especially before you settle down together, is the expectation of a woman doing all the housework and cooking, even if she does not like cooking, does not wish to cook and has no desire to cook! She would rather depend on you or dine out whenever possible! Or, you might have a job that you value but fail to consider the importance to her of *her* job when assuming that she will stay at home and look after the children.

Or take the expectation of one person wanting children while the other does not. It then becomes a major issue of conflict in the relationship, especially when that should have been sorted quite a while back, at the dating stage, in fact. Desires are always changing, but the major ones go on forever. Do remember to know what you want and where you're heading. It will stop an awful lot of misunderstandings, unrealistic expectations and arguments later on.

## Developing Flexibility

There are lots of unhappy people in their relationships at the moment who genuinely believe that the union can never get better because things have gone too far down the road of resentment and animosity. But, so long as some chemistry is still there regarding feelings and emotions, and the frustration and anger can also be communicated and resolved, merely changing expectations a little bit in favour of the other party, and also increasing personal affirmation, can boost many relationships, big time.

Another thing to bear in mind is that people tend to become entrenched in their expectations, always wanting their own way, without really considering what it might mean for the other person, especially if it goes against their values. As every expectation is dictated by a value, the farther apart we are in values from our soulmate, the more frustration there will be when they do not accommodate our expectations, and vice versa.

The best way to deal with expectations on both sides is to make them flexible. NLP authors Steve Andreas and Charles Faulkner[7] suggest that having just one way of resolving anything becomes a straitjacket and makes you 'a robot'. Two ways only and you have a dilemma. But having at least three ways of problem-solving gives you real choice. To achieve that ideal, I believe that every expectation should come in three forms: your way, your soulmate's way and the 'compromising' way, which should itself contain at least three more possible ways to compromise.

However, if you are both only interested in fulfilling your own expectations, then your relationship is likely to be short. For one reason or another, your spouse's choice will not always be desirable, beneficial or inclusive. In fact, it is likely to be perceived as selfish and exclusive. So having expectations that are flexible is the best approach for two people trying to cooperate rather than to compete.

We're heavily influenced by our society, which values flawless performance and places great emphasis upon winning, especially for men. While it is only natural to care about doing the best you can, it is also important to learn to feel good about yourself just for who you are, warts and all; to link your expectations to your fallibility and the desire to enhance others too.

Nothing is ever exactly as you want it, but individual confidence will do much to shape your circumstances to your own satisfaction. This confidence comes from personal power and the inner resources to deal with your life in various unexpected ways that do not compromise others, or put them at a disadvantage.

Individual power and confidence in a relationship are usually based on how well the partners have done in previous situations. "It's probably good to get back to the feeling we had as children, when we had self-confidence without even questioning it. We were valued for being people, for just being born into this world. As adults we often believe we must continually justify our place in the world, especially weaker minorities in a majority community, women in the world of men or people with disabilities among the able-bodied," (Sihera - *Money, Sex & Compromise*[8])

We often believe we have to somehow prove

to other people that we are worthy of their esteem, spending excessive amounts of time worrying about it. In the meantime we lose sight of the basic fact that we are usually fine just as we are and deserve the right to our existence, our identity and whomever we wish to be. This makes us strive to fulfil the impossible expectations of others in a frustrating and futile manner. Result: constant stress, anxiety and feelings of inadequacy.

~~~~~~~~~~~~~~~~~~~~~~~~~~~~~~~~~

### Exercise Six

How have your expectations helped or harmed your relationship or your progress in life? Are your expectations too low, too high, or non-existent? Let's find out.

A. *Return to the three categories of your life: Personal, Relationship and Professional. For each category list your top 10 expectations of them. What must you have now to feel good about each area? What will each fulfilled expectation mean to you?*

B. *What kind of trend is running through them? Are they realistic or weak in impact? Do they centre upon certain elements or are they varied?*

C. *Ask yourself, do they really reflect your heart's desires or are they conforming to someone else's expectations? Would they truly make you happy or are they a mask for something else you do not wish to reveal?*

D. *Select your TOP FIVE expectations in each category. What stands out about them? Match them up against the expectations the significant others in these areas (like your boss) are likely to  have of you. Are there major discrepancies between your expectations and theirs? By the way, if you have no likelihood of ever getting any of these expectations fulfilled, you are in the wrong place!*

Your expectations tell you about your ambitions, your sense of achievement, your satisfaction with yourself, your home, job and your life in general; whether you need more time and experience or whether you are ready now. Do take careful note of them. They are essential signposts to your development and progress, even if they cannot be fulfilled immediately.

Once again, you CANNOT compromise your top five core requirements in any area of your life because they represent the essence of you. Unfulfilled expectations not only cause frustration, anxiety and resentment, they also reinforce your feelings of helplessness and/or incompetence. You will only feel inadequate if they are not satisfied. So work out why you have those expectations and how they can be fulfilled.

By completing the exercise above with some real thought, *10 Easy Steps To....Finding Your Ideal Soulmate!* should help you to establish realistic expectations which can only enhance your experiences.

~~~~~~~~~~~~~~~~~~~~~~~~~~~~~~~~~~~

## REFLECTION
Step Six in *Finding Your Ideal Soulmate....*

### *HAVE REALISTIC EXPECTATIONS!*
.... They are more likely to be fulfilled, thus affirming you as the exciting person you wish to be while ensuring more successful and rewarding interactions with others.

# ~ STEP SEVEN ~

## **Reciprocity: Give And Take**

Carol was complaining bitterly. Her boyfriend of four years never took her anywhere, not even 'to have a meal or see a film'. She felt like a 'skivvy', there only to 'keep house, cook meals and look after the kids'. He always complained of having too much work to do, she said, and the time was never right to take some time off. He was a production manager for a retail firm and there were always some last-minute orders he had to supervise. She felt he was beginning to take her for granted and she had started to feel 'resentful and ignored'. She didn't know why she bothered, she said resignedly, adding that she was 'not going to put up with it anymore'.

Leroy was no different. He felt that though he worked 'all hours God sent' for his family, he received little thanks for it. He loved his wife very much, and was always giving her surprise gifts to show her how he felt and to affirm her value to him, but she never did anything in return, unlike this woman in his office who was 'always trying to do little things' to attract his attention. His wife didn't show him any value, 'never put herself out' for him, and so it felt as though she didn't really love him. He was tired of trying to start conversations that were not just routine, especially when he never received any positive feedback to make the effort worthwhile.

Should he try and get some affirmation elsewhere? he queried. After all, they hardly did anything together because she always had some meeting or other with her job. They were like the proverbial 'ships passing in the night'. He was 'fed up' with her manner but didn't know how to deal with the situation, since he didn't want to make it any worse. But he was 'so frustrated' with feeling invisible, as if he did not matter. He wanted to know if this was what happened when people had been together for 10 years. Did all the romance disappear?

Here are two people in different relationships having identical crises: that of not connecting regularly with their partners on a loving and affirming basis. If the success of relationships could be whittled down to just one word, it would be RECIPROCITY – mutual giving and taking, affirming and reinforcing. Reciprocity is the strongest glue that binds people together. There is nothing greater than mutual reinforcement to remind a couple who they are, where they are coming from, where they are going and what they mean to each other.

## Affirming our Partners

It is always sad to see how partners try to impress one another during dating days, even taking up their hobbies and sports to be near each other, but as soon as the partners settle down and feel secure, they begin to take their soulmates for granted. All the little heartwarming things they used to do for one another, or the sweet little endearments they loved to whisper to each other, gradually peter out and eventually stop altogether. Slowly the relationship becomes a battleground, full of competition, one-upmanship and power struggles, instead of what they should be for – two people loving, appreciating and affirming each other.

It was Susan Jeffers (*Feel the Fear And Do it Anyway*⁹) who said that people who attended her classes found it most difficult to tell their partners something positive and uplifting. Most people had got into such a rut of negativity with their spouses they had forgotten how to be warm, kind, affirming and loving. Some thought their partner didn't 'deserve' such praise or affirmation, as though a relationship was all about punishment and rejection! Others felt that they didn't know how to do it, saying that the words sounded 'odd', while some said their spouses would be suspicious of their new approach and motive and wouldn't really appreciate what they were trying to do.

The tragedy with such a situation is that whatever people are not getting at home, they will gradually seek elsewhere, judging by the millions of men, and many women, currently seeking 'discreet' long-term liaisons – 'no one-night stands' – while their spouses blissfully believe that all is well! That is how David and I met. He was living apart from his wife and felt lonely in the absence of affirmation and reinforcement and I was in the process of leaving my marriage.

The mobile and the Internet have revolutionised what people can do quietly to get what they want when they want it. If only couples remembered that stark fact, then they might make sure that they pulled out all the stops to love and affirm each other.

The essence of any relationship is affirming and reinforcing one another, being there for each other in good and bad times and giving each other the space and understanding to develop as individuals. There is nothing more demoralising than showing someone that he/she is valued but never being reinforced in return, or appreciating your soulmate through praise and support yet never receiving anything back. That sort of one-sided behaviour is a sure killer of motivation and affection in the end.

The three main reasons why we do not affirm and reinforce our loved ones are these:

A. A *lack of reinforcement in childhood*. This leads to low self-esteem and low self-love. This makes it difficult to affirm someone else when we can't even affirm ourselves. We cannot give away what we haven't got, so we tend to take from others instead to compensate for this.

B. *Familiarity and a lack of respect.* We believe the other person doesn't deserve it, for whatever reason, and so we withhold affirmation and reinforcement, once we feel secure about them, in order to boost our egos and as a form of power.

C. *Control of others* by using any kind of positive action as weapons against them. We wait until occasions when they need a word of comfort, a hug, affection or sex and we withhold it as 'punishment' for unseen or past acts. But this eventually leads to a tit-for-tat approach that builds up resentment and anger, ultimately killing any feelings.

## Mutual Reciprocity

Wherever there is an absence of affirmation and reinforcement you will find insecurity, resentment, frustration, control, rejection and unhappiness. It is difficult to feel good about yourself or to thrive in such an environment. In these situations many people become depressed and powerless, especially where children are involved and choices are limited. As a general rule, if someone is not very forthcoming and affirming at the dating stage they will NOT be any better later on because this early stage is when we are at our most affectionate and loving.

If someone seems reticent to give a compliment during dating, reluctant to do things for you, to show any respect and value for you, then it won't suddenly start later on. In fact, it is likely to get worse once you settle and that person feels more comfortable. The tell-tale signs are already there if he/she can't be bothered to make the effort, for example, to look smart for the date, to note your likes and dislikes, to share in activities or to take any interest in your life and work. These are all actions which suggest a single person thinking only of themself.

Mutual reciprocity is the key to appreciating and valuing someone and where it is not in existence there is no foundation to build upon. If you really care about them, if you meant what you said when you were dating or when you

*10 Easy Steps To....*

made vows, and if you really care what happens to the relationship, it takes only a little effort, courage and compassion to affirm that person and make the connection more enriching. This is important because many people are never short of negative comments or criticisms of their dates/partners, so why can't they be equally positive? In fact, it takes just three little words sometimes to repair any emotional damage or make our soulmate feel magnificent.

I have provided a top 10 of three-word statements to help you along, a list sent to me by a friend that I thought I would share with you. It is about being a real friend to others but it applies even more to relationships. Reciprocity was the hallmark of my relationship with David. If I learned nothing else, it was that mutual affirming, loving and supporting was the essence of demonstrating what we meant to each other in both words and deeds. And it easily sustained the passion, excitement and feeling we had between us that developed in a very powerful and enriching way.

## Just Three Words

There are many things that you can do to strengthen your relationships or to show a potential partner the kind of person you are. Often the most effective action involves saying just three little words, nothing else. When spoken sincerely, these statements often have the power to develop new friendships, deepen old ones and even bring healing to relationships that have soured – essential tools for any partnership. I have listed them in my reverse order of priority:

10. *Go for it!*
    This is a most encouraging affirmation that many people long to hear when they wish to create something or start a project. This reinforcement gives added courage. We are all unique individuals, so don't try to get your soulmate to conform to your ideals. Support them in pursuing their own interests, no matter how far-fetched they might appear to you. You are not inside your soulmate's head to see their drive and motivation. Their dreams are unique to them, so support and

encourage your soulmate to follow that dream. The result could be astounding and is likely to be mutually beneficial.

9. *Let me help.*
   Caring soulmates see a need and then try to fill it. When they see a hurt they also do what they can to heal it. Without being asked, they jump in and help out. Why not help your partner to achieve that dream instead of just running it down or ignoring it? It could make a huge difference to them, and even to you.

8. *Count on me.*
   A real friend is one who walks in when others walk out. Loyalty and reliability are essential ingredients for relationships. Being able to count on someone is the greatest form of affirmation and support of others because anyone can be a friend when things are going well. It is when they are bad that you know just how much your soulmate or others appreciate you.

7. *Please forgive me.*
   Many broken relationships could be restored and healed if people would admit their mistakes and ask for forgiveness. But often

they prefer to ignore their fallibility, believing that it is not good to admit they are wrong, that it might make them look bad or rob them of the 'upper hand'. But everyone is vulnerable to faults, foibles and failures.

No one should ever be ashamed to own up that he/she has misjudged a situation. In fact, that's the mark of a leader and maturity: someone willing to take responsibility for their actions. To ask forgiveness for a hurt or wrong word is to acknowledge the gaining of greater wisdom today than you had yesterday. Someone once said that we are either 'green and growing' and ready to learn, or 'ripe and rotting' knowing it all.

Which is it for you?

6. *Maybe you're right.*

This is very effective in diffusing an argument and calming a situation. The implication when you say 'maybe you're right' is the humility of admitting, 'maybe I'm wrong'. It also acknowledges that we don't know everything and that there are always other alternatives available to us.

We can never argue our way into someone agreeing with us. In fact, that is when they are likely to stand their ground since they do

*10 Easy Steps To....*

not wish to lose face. Any argument simply solidifies the other person's point of view and reduces respect. You also run the risk of seriously damaging the relationship. Saying 'maybe you're right' can open the door to explore possibilities. You may then have the opportunity to express your view in a way that is understandable to that person. So, which would you rather be: right, righteous and rejected or amenable, amicable and accepted?

5. *I understand you.*
   Understanding is the basis of respect. You cannot respect what you don't understand because you won't be able to appreciate it, and you cannot love what you don't respect. People become closer and enjoy each other more when the other person understands and accepts them. Letting your spouse know – in  many little ways – that you understand and empathise with them, is one of the most powerful tools for boosting friendships and healing your relationship. It is a great reinforcement for showing value and empathy to another.

4.  *I miss you.*

    Perhaps more relationships could be saved and strengthened if couples simply and sincerely said to each other 'I miss you'. Men, in particular, find this hard to say, because they do not wish to admit their feelings in case it exposes their vulnerability. But this powerful affirmation tells partners they are wanted, needed, desired and loved.

    Consider how important you would feel, if you received an unexpected phone call from your soulmate in the middle of your workday, just to say, 'I miss you and can't wait to see you'. That is a very affirming and inclusive statement that would truly warm your heart. How often have YOU said it to someone in the past week?

3.  *I'll be there.*

    If you have ever had to call a friend in the middle of the night, to take a sick child to hospital, or when your car has broken down some miles from home, you will know how good it feels to hear the statement, 'I'll be there'. Being there for another person is the greatest gift we can give them. But often we are too busy with work or home to be there for our partners. Yet nothing in this world is more important than a human being, especially one close to us. When we are truly present for someone we are renewed in love and friendship. We are restored emotionally and spiritually because being there is at the very core of love and respect.

Thank you so much, Geri, for being there for me on that special day. It meant a lot to me!

2. *I thank you.*

We are constantly seeking something but seldom giving thanks for anything, just taking it for granted as it comes. But gratitude is an exquisite form of courtesy and the essence of our life. If we are mean and ungenerous with any aspect of life, we find it hard to say thanks to anyone, or for anything.

On the other hand, people who enjoy the companionship of close friends and soulmates don't take daily courtesies or actions for granted. They are quick to give gratitude for the many expressions of love they experience. Being thankful is an essential ingredient of fulfilment and success because it ensures that there is always something else to be thankful for. Moreover, people never forget a kindness or a heartfelt 'thank you'.

1. *I respect you.*
   Another way of saying this is 'You are wonderful!' or 'I admire you'. These statements all show one main ingredient – RESPECT – and respect is another way of showing love. We cannot love what we don't respect so where this key element is missing there really is no true love. It would be a superficial and cynical relationship. Respect demonstrates that your soulmate is a true equal and this also applies to all relationships. We cannot have what we haven't earned, so often when we think we have been denied respect, it is because we haven't given any either.

● And in a class of its own.... *I love you.*
   Perhaps the three most important words you can say to your soulmate, yet so many people find them difficult to utter. Telling someone that you truly love them satisfies a person's deepest emotional needs and lies at the heart of reciprocity – their need to belong, to feel appreciated, desired and wanted. Your spouse, your children, your friends and yourself, all need to hear those three little words as often as possible: 'I love you, and you're so special!'

   Love is a choice, it is not just an emotion. So

when we stop saying 'I love you', that's a powerful message of negativity we are sending out. It means that we have stopped loving ourselves too because we cannot be angry or meanspirited with someone else and be happy and fulfilled at the same time! All that we will have inside of us is animosity for as long as we choose to withhold our love. We find happiness only through love and affirmation, through a simple reciprocity of feeling.

~~~~~~~~~~~~~~~~~~~~~~~~~~~~~~~~~~

### *Exercise Seven*

So what is the reciprocity like in your relationship? Whether you have been together for a long or short time, how are you both perceiving and affirming one another? The exercise below should give some clues. Take some paper and answer the questions below. If your partner can do it as well, that's even better, since you can then compare notes.

A. *What six characteristics do you find most appealing in your partner?*

B. *If NONE, what did you find MOST appealing when you first met?*

Finding Your Ideal Soulmate!                    191

C. My partner's main weaknesses are_

D. My partner's main strengths are_

E. Itemise up to five of the BEST things your partner does now.

F. How often do you PRAISE and affirm each other? Daily? Monthly? Not at all?

G. When was the last time you affirmed him/her with something positive? How recent is this?

There should be a visible trend in your answers. They will either be broadly negative or broadly positive. When you remember the negatives easily, and you have difficulty spotting the good points or strengths of your soulmate, there is unlikely to be much reciprocity. The focus would be just on their weaknesses and what is lacking, not on the whole person – a recipe for disaster. By the way, this is an excellent exercise for sorting issues with your children, or significant others in your life, to assess how you treat them.

We only reciprocate when we feel valued and affirmed. So, if you are finding it hard to focus upon your soulmate's strengths, and vice versa, it is because you are seeking scapegoats for your perceived failures and the wrongs in your

*10 Easy Steps To....*

relationship. Something urgently needs to be done to restore the balance. Perhaps honestly talking to one another about the root causes of your feelings instead of being resentful might help.

A relationship is supposed to be a haven from the brickbats in the world around you. A lack of reciprocity in it leaves both parties feeling useless, unwanted and inadequate – feelings you can easily get elsewhere, such as in the workplace or from your community! You don't need them in your relationship as well!

~~~~~~~~~~~~~~~~~~~~~~~~~~~~~~~~~~~~

## REFLECTION

Step Seven in *Finding Your Ideal Soulmate*....

### PRACTISE RECIPROCITY OF ACTION!

.... You will be giving and receiving every day of your life. It will affirm you both as a caring couple and you will feel truly wonderful for it – like significant, appreciated, valued, cherished and desirable human beings.

# ~ STEP EIGHT ~

## **Honesty & Integrity**

**E**veryone values honesty and truth. It makes us feel more comfortable, less vulnerable and even more confident in dealing with others. Honesty is a key requirement for us at all times and we tend to be upset if we discover any dishonesty associated with those we love or care about. Honesty is an excellent value to cultivate and is essential to the success of any relationship, but we are often more demanding of it in others than we are in ourselves. We tend to believe that so long as we expect honesty from others, that proves our own integrity and we do not really have to practise it too! In short, we value the honesty of others while studiously ignoring our own.

Take Carl, a sales manager, who has been unhappily married for some years with three children under 15. Having had a couple of 'bad' relationships, he dislikes women 'who play games or lie or cheat', and does not wish to hurt anyone, least of all his children. He believes honesty matters to him above all else. However, even though he is married, he is secretly seeking someone on a website 'for discreet mutual pleasure without hurting anyone'. Somehow his honesty does not stretch to his current relationship.

His honesty is not applicable to himself in acknowledging the problems within his marriage and finding a genuine solution of some kind that involves both parties in open discussion and negotiation. His honesty also appears incapable of accommodating his current feelings of loneliness enough to actually do something about them in the long-term – actions that might positively affect the rest of his life and give meaning to it.

In fact, his honesty seems to remain only as an ideal in his head, not affecting his actual actions in any way. Otherwise he would approach his problems in a more open manner that shows respect both for himself and the people he cares about. He says he gets 'no love or attention' in his relationship and that he and his wife live 'separate' lives, but one gets the feeling that his wife might be unaware of that 'separation'! And even if it is true, would their living separately make it acceptable for his wife to begin an affair too?

The trouble with also seeking a lover to make everything better, is that another person is being used purely for personal gratification in a dishonest way without any regard to their needs. That lover will never know the real truth of what is going on at home. This in turn then limits her choices, when dealing with someone like Carl, in ways that could be more beneficial to her.

## Tell-tale Signs of Unhappiness

Like many men in his situation, Carl sees no discrepancy between his belief in honesty and his dishonest approach to resolving the issues in his relationship. He feels that in trying to make the best of his situation by 'getting a lover' he is exercising the most sensible option that will cause 'the least problems and hurt'. As he perceives it, this action would benefit him in three ways. It would 'not really hurt anyone', his wife would be 'none the wiser', and he would not have to uproot himself 'to start a new home life' away from his children, especially as he is 'broadly happy' with the way things are. Except that Carl looks anything but happy. He is visibly overweight, weighing at least 230 lbs, he works long hours to affirm himself and he looks very sad and unhappy in his face and manner, three sure signs of distress within a relationship.

When we accept unhappiness as routine, we believe there will be nothing better for us and that we don't deserve anything else. Our self-love gradually diminishes. Work and/or food or something else compensate for the sense of worth and value we have lost. We become workaholics and the weight goes on faster than you can say "more chocolates", developments that, of course, make the person even less appealing to himself and others.

When we are unhappy, we also tend to care only about our own needs. As a result, neither his wife nor the new lover Carl is seeking would be treated with any respect, except as means to an end. So long as he is 'discreet', he says, everything should be fine. But his own fears for his future, and his inability or reluctance to take some effective action about it, ensure that his honesty goes out of the window, adding even more stress to his pain and discomfort. Of course, stress is the worst thing one can possibly live with on a daily basis.

## Lowering Personal Standards

Alternatively, consider Myrna, who is the high-powered director of her own company. She has been in a long-term relationship for 12 years, one that makes her deeply unhappy. She readily admits to having had 'no affection, no love and no sex for years' from her very successful partner. There are no children of the union but she enjoys an affluent lifestyle that she does not wish to lose so she puts up with a demoralising, unloving and non-reinforcing situation continuously for material gains. She complains of feeling 'undervalued, unloved and lonely' most of the time, while her high-flying husband openly dates other women.

She too values honesty and believes she is a 'very honest person'. But she drifts from one relationship to another seeking sex and affirmation to compensate for her unexciting life, yet without really finding the kind of love and reinforcement she seeks because she is living in an indecisive and unfulfilling manner that goes against her own integrity and decisiveness. Her dishonest way of life is at odds with how she wishes to be perceived and valued; a feeling that can only get worse as her liaisons become even less fulfilling.

From the time she began to ignore or repress her emotions of unhappiness and rejection, Myrna began to move away from her values of honesty and to lose her own integrity. She refuses to face her situation because she feels she 'cannot afford' to do otherwise. Being in her 50s, and despite being well-off, she believes she is 'too old' to do anything else at this stage. She fears 'not having enough money' and 'having to start all over again when nothing is perfect'. And so she stays put, feeling secure in one way but very unhappy, frustrated and loveless in another, always seeking external attention to boost her self-esteem. However, the more we

*10 Easy Steps To....*

compromise the honesty we believe in, the more difficult it is to be true to ourselves, to be truly honest with others and to live with any kind of integrity and contentment. We are not living up to our own standards so it is difficult for anyone to trust us or to take us seriously. Soon the lies pile up so high that it becomes easier to add yet another lie to maintain our position than to unravel them all and be whom we wish to be in an open and honest manner.

Dishonesty is often due to a reluctance to pay the price for our beliefs. We wish to live in a certain way, to find the ultimate happiness we seek. But happiness comes at a price and too often we sacrifice it for convenience, choosing to live in frustration, fear and misery – a kind of quiet, slow death of the spirit, in fact.

Honesty is about sincerity and respect. Like charity, it begins at home, with one's self first. We cannot be honest with others if we lie to ourselves, if we deny our personal needs and desires, if we pretend to be one thing when we are actually another and if honesty is expected of others while we ignore it in ourselves. Honesty is a core value that dictates how we view the world and how we respond to it. We cannot respond honestly if our perception of our world is dishonest.

For, example, if you believe that your husband is cheating on you but have no proof and feel powerless to discuss it, that perception and lack of action will lead to dishonest ways of confirming your belief. However, if you believe he could be cheating and you are prepared to confront both him and yourself about the reasons for that action, you would have begun the process of honestly tackling the situation and of resolving it in a more beneficial and empowering way.

No one leaves steak at home for lesser cuts outside, so if one party is being unfaithful, both parties need to examine themselves. Naturally, if he continues to lie about a situation you 'know' to be true, there is nothing you can do except live that lie with him and reinforce it. But, better still, you could change your own behaviour in order to benefit yourself, an action that will empower you and inevitably change your situation in the long-term.

## Honesty and Respect

We all value honesty to a large extent but honesty is tied up with respect. Respect for oneself, in particular, which then extends to respect for others. When we are dishonest to ourselves or others we are not holding ourselves in the high esteem we crave. Soon we will begin to feel worse as our self-esteem plummets and we become vulnerable to being 'found out'.

When we have little respect for someone's feelings, whether that is because they are weak, controlling or not in alignment with us, we are more likely to be dishonest with them. The main problem with that action is that it continually denies and represses what we ourselves seek. Sometimes it might seem easier and less painful to hide the truth from our partners, but such dishonesty tends to have a cumulative effect that becomes ever harder to resolve as new lies are added. Worse still, such dishonesty is usually found out in the end, and often when we least expect it, precipitating exactly what we feared.

For example, many people in partnerships will say that they prefer to 'stay together for the children's sake' while living a lie to protect them. But this is a BAD idea. Children learn from their parents, and especially from their actions, not their words. The only thing they are learning during that time of silent animosity, dishonesty and pretence, is how to be dishonest themselves, how to live with constant pain and without acknowledgement. They are learning to regard living like robots, without love and affirmation, as some kind of honourable act!

Above all, the children are learning how to live loveless lives of quiet desperation in order to keep up appearances. Not only will the silence reinforce the feeling that they are in some way responsible for their parents' situation, but, as there is no end to it until they leave home, it will negatively affect their own perception of others and their relationships too. In the absence of any other models, they will believe that this is the way 'normal' parents behave. Better to have one loving parent who can affirm that child daily than to have two quietly warring factions thriving on dishonesty and setting the worst kind of example to their children.


Finally, a word of warning about affairs: NEVER

disclose an affair to your partner *after* it has finished! Best to let sleeping dogs lie in case they wake up and bite you! In those circumstances you might believe that you are being 'honest' and that it will clear the air for a better relationship. Sadly it never does. Trust goes immediately while the perception of your dishonesty becomes magnified and solidified for the future. You are also not really being 'honest' at all, otherwise you would have disclosed it at the beginning of the affair. Often when we confess past affairs it is to assuage our own guilt, not because we care about our partner's feelings.

Most importantly, though mere mortals might want 'the truth', they cannot deal with imagining their partners enjoying love and sex with another while they have been neglected or rejected. At such times, they are likely to focus upon your actions – especially the salacious bits – which will seem very selfish and painful, not on the root causes of why you sought solace in the first place. So, resist the temptation to confess and let it quietly go. This is a case where ignorance is definitely bliss! As long as there is no repetition, and you use it to improve your relationship, you will have a better chance of continuing harmony.

## Dishonesty During Dating

People who are dating tend to be the worst offenders as regards not being honest about themselves, and this certainly tends to result in unforeseen repercussions later on. The anonymity of the Internet, in particular, encourages such dishonesty among people trying hard to impress. Often people have pictures of 'themselves' on websites that are significantly out of date, air-brushed to make them look more glamorous than they are, or even pictures of completely different people! Or they will say that they are slimmer, taller or younger than they appear in their profile, forgetting that they might very well meet someone they fancy at some later stage and that truth will out.

If you can get away with appearing much younger and do not wish to be treated in an ageist manner, being 'economical with the truth' about your age is acceptable to some extent, so long as you are honest about it face-to-face. Age is how you think about your life, your whole attitude and approach to it, and not

*10 Easy Steps To....*

just the number.

I advocate this because men, in particular, write off most women who have reached 50, as if that age changes them into ogres or alien beings who have no further use! In those cases, some education is necessary, I think, to help such people face their fears. I remember once putting that I was 48 on a website and getting a lot of replies. I changed the details just two months later to my real age of 55 and got not a single response. Yet I used the same profile in every respect, including the same pictures! Being over 50 instantly propelled me out of their preferred age range.

So age is a different category in trying to reach people because of our innate fears and prejudices about the ageing process. But lying about other aspects of yourself, when everyone can clearly see that you are shorter or much bigger than you claim to be, is not a good start to a relationship.

When we are dishonest it is because we are either seeking approval from others we fear or wish to impress, we fear the consequences of our actions and opt for convenience and a quiet life, or we feel embarrassed by acknowledging the real truth of our situation. But the sign of a mature person is the willingness to take responsibility for our actions in a fearless way. This will then mark us as someone worth dealing with and respecting.

If we are proud of who we are, if we see ourselves as the only person responsible for our actions and have no need or wish for someone else's approval in order to be ourselves, then there is no need to be dishonest in our search for a soulmate or in other aspects of our lives. We would wish to start with the truth in all aspects and be treated with honesty too in return. It lays the foundation for mutual respect and establishes the right open foundation for that relationship from the first time both parties meet.

As James Allen (*As A Man Thinketh*[10]) wrote, "Men do not attract what they seek. They attract who they are." Quite simply, it means to be careful how you act, because your actions will be returned to you in triplicate! If we are dishonest, we will only attract equally dishonest people.

But if you live with integrity, most people around you will reflect that integrity too and value you even more for it.

~~~~~~~~~~~~~~~~~~~~~~~~~~~~~~~~~~~~

### *Exercise Eight*

How honest are you to yourself, to your date or to soulmate? Are there issues that are preventing your own honesty from coming to the fore? Try the exercises below, especially if you are in a relationship.

1.A. *Do you have any major secrets from your partner right now? List up to five of the most important ones.*

B. *How does keeping them hidden make you feel each day?*

C. *How do your feelings connect to your happiness rating in Step One?*

D. *Why do you feel you cannot disclose them?*

E. *What is the worst thing that would happen to you if you actually discussed them with your soulmate?*

F. *How does that compare to carrying a burden of stress and dishonesty for the rest of your time together?*

2. How many of the items below do you really FEAR at this moment? Award between zero and five points for the level of fear you feel for each of

them RIGHT now – (five means that you are very afraid, zero means that you feel no fear, and three means that you are neither fearful nor fearless concerning each item).

A. *FAILURE*

B. *Loss of LOVE*

C. *Being HURT in a Relationship*

D. *POVERTY*

E. *DEATH*

F. *ILL-HEALTH*

G. *COMMITMENT*

H. *Getting OLDER*

I. *CRITICISM*

J. *Being ALONE or ISOLATED*

What is your score? If you scored more than 15 then you are probably finding it difficult to live honestly because your fears are preventing you from facing up to truths about your unhappiness and dealing with them in ways which would render those fears less threatening.

For example, if you really fear item J (*Being Alone or Isolated*) you would try to avoid that at all costs, even when you are in emotional pain and being treated badly by your partner. You will choose to lie to yourself and to minimise or play down your feelings. You are likely to do anything to remain in that situation in order to prevent yourself from being lonely and isolated. However, once you realise that, until you love yourself first and do not mind being alone with yourself, no one will be able to love you, then being alone will no longer be such an issue for you. You will lose your fear of isolation and appreciate your life on a more meaningful basis.

You will recognise that to be alone is not the same as being lonely. It is actually essential self-affirmation and acceptance. As your fear of rejection recedes, seeking ways to be happier, both within yourself and with others, will gradually become a greater priority in your life. You will love yourself so much you will not tolerate unhappiness just to avoid being lonely.

It is our fear of death and loss of love that paralyses us and prevents us from making the most of the life we have. Once we appreciate that certain things like loss of love, ageing and death are inevitable, we then begin to recognise just how powerful we are in making our life what we wish in the brief time we have, not what someone else dictates for us. That sets the foundation for being honest both to ourselves and to those who matter to us.

~~~~~~~~~~~~~~~~~~~~~~~~~~~~~~~~~

## REFLECTION

Step Eight in *Finding Your Ideal Soulmate....*

### *PRACTISE HONESTY AND INTEGRITY!*

.... Your actions will be transparent and you will gain both your own respect and that of others in living the life you choose.

\* \* \* \* \* \*

*What counts in making a happy relationship
is not so much how compatible you are,
but how you deal with incompatibility.*

Daniel Goleman

# ~ STEP NINE ~

## <u>Respect</u>

O n its own, this step could make or break a relationship. In fact, the word RESPECT runs throughout this book, popping up in every chapter. However, the reason why it is so low in the pecking order is because you have to be with someone for a certain amount of time before you can work out whether they have true respect for you or not. Sometimes you are fortunate to find out literally within days of meeting him/her (like I did!). At other times it could take years because of the different stages in a partnership and the habits we develop.

Once I met a very pleasant man (I thought) with great chemistry between us. I was really excited at the possibilities for us until he broke FIVE promises in the first four days: two relating to phoning me (he didn't), the other three regarding his help with simple things which mattered to me (which he never gave). I let him go, reluctantly, soon afterwards because he was violating my top value of being treated with respect. Would you break off what seemed like a 'great' relationship for the sake of broken promises? Especially if they seem to be trivial ones? Perhaps you wouldn't, but I would – anytime.

If it starts with broken promises it really does not get any better. It is all about respect and the priority you are given, as well as the trust you have in that person to keep their word. Furthermore, if a person starts by reneging on the little things, then the big things are usually not far behind.

I am always reinforcing the people who matter to me. If I care about them, they deserve to know how I feel, and vice versa. So I get a particular thrill from acknowledging them, celebrating and reinforcing them as they are, and treating them with the utmost respect. I ring them often, wish them well on their days, praise and compliment them routinely and love to

Finding Your Ideal Soulmate!

hear about their activities. That is because I value them and feel they are significant to my life.

If that person does not reciprocate in most ways, I leave him alone. You are not there to make people into what you want or seek. They deserve the respect of being who they are too. Your priority is to find someone who matches your approach enough to make you feel great and to reinforce whom you wish to be. That is why I would rather halt a budding friendship than continue with it and then nag that person into submission. That is not fair to either of us. We all have to be ourselves. It is gross insecurity and a desire to control that makes us seek to change others in major ways in order to match our ideal.

## Promises and Priorities

A promise is the essence of respect because it carries the implication of the VALUE we place on a person within it. If we value our soulmates, we appreciate them and they come at the top of our priorities – every time. They might not always

*10 Easy Steps To....*

be Number One, depending on the context and the demands, but they will always matter above most other things.

When people promise to call, for instance, yet never find the time to phone, or leave all the calling to you without it being reciprocal; or when they put work before you constantly, and when they even have to think before they can accommodate you, they are sending a BIG message about your value and their respect for you – and you ignore it at your peril. How long does it take to send a text message with seven words saying "Very busy...call later...thinking of you."? That's a five-second job for the fast texters among us. It might take 30 seconds for mere mortals, but it is still only a few seconds long.

If you have recently met someone who cannot spare you 30 seconds when they break their promise, it is already time to ditch them. Believe me, it will be far less painful now than when it becomes a definite pattern and you gradually find out just how low you really are in their order of priorities. Leaders and genuine carers keep their promises because they are tied to integrity and honesty. That also guarantees success through enhanced reputation.

Spike made a promise to Fallon whom he had met a couple times and fancied. He would ring her as soon as he got in from work that day, he proposed. She was secretly pleased at his interest and waited eagerly for his call. They were just getting to know each other and she was keen to have contact to see where it would lead. But just before he was due to ring her, he got another call and was distracted by it. Fallon lost out because he forgot. He texted her to apologise and suggested another call for the next day. However, he was busy calling so many other friends he forgot her again. He also believed in the 'treat 'em mean and keep 'em keen' approach. Only Fallon didn't know that!

This time she sent a text message to remind him that he hadn't called twice. He said he forgot, apologised again but then complained of feeling 'hassled'. He made a third promise which he did not keep either because he had to go out. That last broken promise did it for her. Fallon assumed he was not worth it and stopped waiting. She had lost her respect for, and trust in, him. He also didn't call her again either because he felt guilty.

This was a golden opportunity wasted.

*10 Easy Steps To....*

## Promises and Respect

Promises mean a lot to people because they suggest appreciation, value and empathy and carry some pleasure in fulfilment. Above all they suggest RESPECT. The effect of broken promises is undue anxiety, resentment, missed opportunities and a lack of trust in future promises for the aggrieved party, as well as a chain of guilt and feelings of incapacity and/or inadequacy for the other. Furthermore, a promise often prevents those to whom it is given from taking alternative action, which means everyone loses out all round. Finally, if not handled sensitively, broken promises can cause ill feeling, damage friendships and even lose business.

A promise to someone is all about respect and trust because it says: "I value and appreciate you. You are significant to me and I want to do something with, or for, you to get a particular thrill from doing it and seeing the result. You also trust me to do it according to my word and I won't betray that trust." We all have moments when we make a promise to someone and cannot keep it, for a variety of urgent and unexpected reasons to do with our circumstances. That is understandable, so long as it only happens sporadically. However, when there is a definite pattern of broken promises it suggests three things:

1. That the person to whom the promise is made isnot really a priority in the scheme of things, and is certainly not as valued as others.

2. That the person making the promise is trying to please too many people at once, perhaps to impress, but failing miserably.

3. That the promise itself is not perceived as important enough to be kept and was perhaps made for show, or to reinforce or enhance a reputation.

These three reasons suggest that genuine action needs to be taken to avoid future hurt. Most people don't mind the odd broken promise – we are all guilty of it – but if it becomes a pattern then it becomes part of our personality and is a pointer to how we treat others in order to maintain our own feelings of comfort and power. It really does not suggest enough respect for the person on the receiving end, not to mention that it would also be irritating for them. Breaking promises to me was a pattern for that guy I broke off with, especially as it applied just to me and him, no one else.

As far as I knew, he could have been keeping all his promises to some other person he valued more. Indeed, this might even have been what prevented him keeping the ones he made to me. So one can never assume that such behaviour is being applied to others, a fact that increases its importance between the two people involved because it goes right to the heart of respect.


## The Five Dimensions of Respect

Respect is demonstrated by our actions, not by our words, and when those actions are absent, especially at a trivial or simple level, there is also a distinct lack of respect. For example, in every relationship respect goes hand-in-hand with love and commitment.

You cannot love someone you don't respect or are not prepared to commit to, even for a short time. Otherwise you will resent the time spent with them, or spent doing things on their behalf, when you could be doing something else or be with someone else. Neither can you love someone you really do not trust. Once trust is gone, the feelings become superficial as the relationship shifts in terms of both emotion and power. You would no longer respect that person, tending to be suspicious of their actions instead of celebrating and enjoying their presence.

We also use the word 'respect' very glibly but without really understanding it fully. Respect is not just one term. It carries five other dimensions within it:

1. curiosity
2. attention
3. dialogue
4. empowerment
5. healing

If we are not really demonstrating these five concepts with regards to the one we say we respect, we are not showing them much respect at all. We are simply paying lip-service.

1. *Curiosity*

   Respect starts with curiosity. We have an interest in that person. We want to know something about them, at least a few key things to start with. In the dating process we engineer all kinds of opportunities to satisfy that curiosity and are often mortified when we get no response from our interest and cannot fulfil that curiosity in any way. We feel frustrated and insignificant.

2. *Attention*

   If curiosity is satisfied, we move to give that person our full attention. Indeed, our curiosity grows too because that person begins to assume value in our eyes. The amount of value will depend on the way they satisfy our curiosity and attention. If the information we get is weak, unappealing or non-reinforcing, we lose interest rapidly, our attention wanes and we move towards another. However, if we perceive that the new interest aligns with us and matches us in major ways, excitement and interest both quicken. We then lavish even more attention on that person, going out of our way to attract their attention and interest on a more intense level.

3. *Dialogue*

Lots of attention inevitably leads to much dialogue because that is the only way we can learn about our new interest. We communicate verbally as much as possible because we respect that person enough to want to hear what they have to say. We also take the greatest pleasure in conversing for its own sake. Hence much money will be spent on dates and on phone calls, in particular. Where there is little respect, we are not in the least bit interested in that person and won't even talk to them. If there is also disrespect, for example, made through assumptions about them based upon their gender, colour, sexuality etc., we are likely to treat them negatively. Any dialogue at such times will only express our anxieties, prejudices, resentment or anger, not our respect.

4. *Empowerment*

Being curious about someone, giving them our attention and having a dialogue with him or her represent the greatest form of empowerment we can grant to another human being. Empowerment is awesome because that person gains SELF-RESPECT in the

*10 Easy Steps To....*

process, as well as the self-belief that everything is possible and they are valued and cherished. When we lose respect, our self-esteem and confidence go with it too. So there is no greater emotion than respecting someone. Through respect we demonstrate to him/her that we like what we see and, in essence, we want them to love, affirm and accept themself. In essence, we empower them too. Thus respect is crucial for positive personal development.

Most people simply wish to please the significant others they care about. When that is reciprocated with obvious respect, it says a great deal about their value, the relationship itself and the interaction. For example, if someone is trying to talk to you but you are busy playing on your computer, or talking to someone else on the phone, that shows little reciprocity for the respect they might be giving to you. So whenever anyone says that they are 'too busy' to see you because they have 'so much to do', especially in business terms, that should be the biggest pointer for you as to the level of your value in their eyes. If they valued you more, they would have moved mountains to accommodate you!

5. *Healing*

Respect has the capacity to heal, especially when we have had past experiences that have been very hurtful or traumatic, so this last dimension is very important. When we have had a bad time it is very affirming to be respected and valued by the new person we are attracted to, or the people we interact with, and it is most effective in speeding up the healing process. When we heal we empower. We affirm that person enough to show them what is possible.

For example, if someone felt really inadequate because his woman went off with a younger, more handsome man, a new lover in his life, demonstrating how wonderful he is, would give him much-needed respect and reinforcement. This would help to heal his pain even quicker than if he had to overcome it by himself. Respect heals because it affirms and reinforces who we are and wish to be. It also puts past hurt in perspective, or even negates it, and thus restores our confidence.

Altogether these five dimensions add up to the powerful concept of respect and when we show another human being that respect and trust, we add an even greater experience to their life and perspectives. We are all empowered by its effects.

Respect and trust can never be taken for granted. They have to be earned because they are attributes that have to be proven. They are also directly reciprocal to the behaviour of others. For example, when we feel that we have had no respect from the people we care about, it is likely that we have given them very little respect ourselves. Most of us are sensitive to when we are not being treated with respect and are unable to give any in it's absence.

If you feel disrespected, what are you doing in the process? There is always a connection. You are either accepting substandard behaviour in order to gain approval, or you are not treating someone else well enough. Once you sort out the root cause of your feelings and actions toward others, mutual respect and trust are usually assured.

~~~~~~~~~~~~~~~~~~~~~~~~~~~~~~~~~~~~

### *Exercise Nine*

How much do you respect and trust your soulmate or your date? Rate the level out of 10. If you haven't given a full 10, what is keeping you from awarding it? 'No one is perfect' is not an acceptable reason here! Make a list of the causes. You need to examine all the reasons why you would not give full points because they will need to be addressed. Even if you believe your fears are unfounded, they will still need to be faced, otherwise they will only grow stronger and cause resentment.

On the other side of the coin, how might your date or spouse rate you on this aspect? What rating might you be given, and why? It should be interesting to find out and compare notes, especially if there is a discussion about the ratings and how they could be improved, where necessary.


A lack of trust and respect stems from resentment and grows slowly into a sense of injustice and then anger. You can see it immediately in broken promises or the reluctance to put oneself out for that other person. It really cannot be ignored. By nurturing respect in your relation-

228                              *10 Easy Steps To....*

ship, or by starting out with it on your dates, you stand the best chance of being treated with respect yourself and of the relationship growing with much love and trust. There is no other way.

~~~~~~~~~~~~~~~~~~~~~~~~~~~~~~~~~~~

## REFLECTION

Step Nine in *Finding Your Ideal Soulmate*....

### *GIVE GENUINE RESPECT!*

.... You will not only make the other person feel fabulous, you will also feel great too because you will be reinforcing each other in an appreciative, a valued and a significant way

✳ ✳ ✳ ✳ ✳ ✳

*The easiest thing to find is fault. It takes no thought, no talent, no creativity and no action.*

Elaine Sihera

# ~ STEP TEN ~

## **Commitment & Trust**

How many times have you met someone you are getting on really well with, feeling great about, and then she wants to strengthen the relationship, to make it more permanent. You suddenly start recoiling in horror and you come out in a cold sweat at the thought of it (like David felt with me). The hairs on the back of your neck stand upright in fright and you begin to retreat from her. You emphasise that all you wanted was 'friendship', yet everything you were doing is well beyond the 'friendship' stage and your new 'friend' is now getting impatient. She cannot understand your reaction because the suggestion seems to be a natural development. You begin to worry about all the possible things that could go wrong to 'spoil' what you have now and you back off, expecting to be able to resume where you left off. But it is likely to be the end of that beautiful friendship because you fear to commit, or you keep putting it off for no clear reason.

You have changed the situation through your fear, and once you are seen in that negative light, having revealed that apparent 'commit-ment phobia' to your friend, things can never return to normal. The relationship will either remain in limbo, as your soulmate adjusts to your reaction, it will fall apart rapidly or it will die a gradual death.

And then you're back to square one, wondering why everything tends to end like that. You are unlikely to believe that your lack of commitment had anything to do with it. Instead, you will assume that the other person was being unreasonable in their expectations, thanking your lucky stars that you got out just in time!

✳ ✳ ✳ ✳ ✳ ✳

*Argue for your limitations, and sure enough, they're yours!*

Richard Bach

*10 Easy Steps To....*

## Enrichment and Joy

The most important word behind love and respect is commitment. This trio of words is crucial to any relationship, no matter how brief. When we respect or love someone, we commit to her or him for whatever time required in the interaction. That's the price we pay for more happiness with someone else. We commit to affirming them, aligning with them, to reinforcing their aspirations and self-belief, to valuing them as a significant person we admire and to enhancing their happiness while expanding our own.

Through commitment comes enrichment and joy. So when we cannot commit to another person, we are only half alive, existing without the contentment we seek. It is fine to be alone and single for the rest of one's life, but that means settling for so much less than is possible in this world.

Human value comes from interaction, affirmation and love. If we are not reinforced in any way, we are likely to feel excluded from the social contact we crave. Our life becomes joyous only when we are enriched by someone else, and vice versa. We do not need anyone to complete us physically, but we do need others to enrich the quality of our lives, if we are not to become mechanical robots with fossilised emotions. People give meaning and purpose to our lives. Without them we feel invisible.

There are many reasons for not being able to commit to another person in a new friendship, but the main one is an inability to let go of the past. We either keep past partners in a 'halo effect' and no one is allowed to match them, or we demonise them and derogate their actions. Even though the past is gone and we cannot go back there to change anything, we tend to cling to it like limpets, reliving the old horrible memories and judging every new interaction by them, seeking scapegoats for the continuing pain. But using the past to judge the present only deprives us of a future and a mate.

Sometimes it is not enough to blame past partners for our experience so the blame spreads to all men (or all women), who then become demons in our eyes. We fear a repeat of our hurt so the next person we meet suffers from our pain without knowing what they have done. They are then deprived of the commitment they rightfully deserve. Men are particularly guilty of this. Often a man will tell the next woman who treats him well that she has 'restored' his faith in women, as if the one woman who caused his pain represented the whole gender species!

Commitment is possible only when we can face our past and leave it behind; when we actually learn from our mistakes, accept our fallibility and are prepared to seize new opportunities that present themselves to us. All four steps go together so that when we find it hard to forgive and move on, to learn from our honest mistakes or to look on the brighter side of life, we are then unable to make use of all the chances life regularly presents us with.

Our view of life becomes lop-sided as we focus mainly upon the negatives and avoid the positives. This is why we are reluctant to regard a new relationship with joy and to give thanks for someone special coming into our life. Instead, we view it with fear and trepidation that, of course, it could all go wrong!

## Killing Confidence and Motivation

Past experiences mould us, so when people keep dwelling on the hurt or regretting the failures of the past it means they are always living back there and are not learning anything new. Sometimes it is difficult to escape from the past because of an incident that was so hurtful we keep looking back on it in a vain attempt to resolve it. But once we have passed a given point we cannot return to it. We kill our confidence if we dwell upon past actions by constantly dredging up painful memories or bottling-up hurtful feelings, because the only place that event is still taking place is inside our head. Nowhere else. We are then too occupied fretting about what happened instead of thinking positively of what we could do to change things for the better TODAY.

To surround yourself with nothing but past, hurtful memories merely kills motivation, and robs you of a present and a life, making you very unattractive in the process. It also makes you unhappy and you are likely to carry that misery around like a heavy necklace without even realising the toll it is taking on you.

We often refuse to openly acknowledge our pain because we prefer to see another person as the sole cause of it. We might find it difficult to readily accept responsibility for our actions since that would cause discomfort. But, in any relationship, it takes two for everything to happen. Unless we acknowledge our part in it, and use it to forgive and forget, we will be locked on a path of anger, inactivity and resentment for a very long time.

Eventually bitter, resentful thoughts bury us in negativity and prevent us from taking advantage of the positive things that will grace our lives. This usually leads to difficulties in committing to others as our fear levels are high and we would focus upon the 'bad' things that are likely to happen instead of the wonderful things that could come out of merging with another person in a new experience. That is living well below our capacity and a waste of our precious time.

\* \* \* \* \* \*

*You, yourself, as much as anybody in the entire universe, deserve your love and affection.*

Buddha

## The Need to Blame Others

The inability to learn from our past stems from the desire to always blame someone else for our pain. But, unless someone abducts us against our will, or we are under age, as adults we are responsible for every single decision and action that we take. No one 'makes' us do anything. It is our reaction to others that dictates how we feel and the consequences that follow.

For example, Carter and Sunita had been dating for six months. He was getting bored and frustrated with her reluctance to take things further so he decided to accept an invitation from another girl to a party in order to 'spice things up'. He deliberately chose the party where he knew Sunita would be, pretending that he didn't know she was there.

Sunita was surprised to see them and felt humiliated at his action. She lashed out at the other girl, blaming Carter for her reaction. If he hadn't bought the girl to the party, she argued, she would not have felt angry enough to slap her. But Sunita's action could only be blamed on Sunita. She had the choices – either to ignore

*10 Easy Steps To....*

the pair, to be friendly until she and Carter were alone, or to be angry in order to express her hurt feelings.

She chose the one she desired the most. It had little to do with Carter and everything to do with how she felt she needed to respond to save face. Unless Sunita  accepts her part in the scene, she will continue to blame her boyfriend for everything that happens from then on.

Often, particularly with relationships that we believe have 'failed', we may try to perpetuate the notion that the past was much worse than it was. We isolate only the ghastly bits, exaggerate the bad times, demonise past partners, and pretend that nothing good existed in a past friendship. Yet, even if everything really was awful, the fact that we have survived that period has made us far better beings and infinitely more resilient. We would have learned lots from the past for which we should be grateful. Furthermore, that person ALWAYS enriches our life in some way, otherwise we would not have teamed up with them at all!

By being cynical and distrustful of the world around us we alienate ourselves, lose our confidence and make our environment more frightening. We also deny ourselves the real pleasure we can get from having new experiences to make our lives more fulfilling and enjoyable. Worse still, we are deprived of contact and interaction with new people who could enrich our life, teach us something new and also heal our pain.

When we cannot commit to others, it not only shows a lack of trust in ourself, but we are actually unable to commit to life itself because we miss many of the opportunities that could make it so much better.

## Enjoying the Ride

Commitment to life means seizing the opportunities that come your way. When you find a soulmate, it is not for you to ask how long it will last, to dwell on when there will be a break-up or to wonder whether the person will be in your life forever or just for now. The only thing you are required to do at that first moment of realisation is to give thanks that someone wonderful has come into your life. Just sit back and enjoy the ride without questioning its credibility or longevity. Allow it to unfold around you in an exciting and surprising way. You will be amazed at what is possible. It is our desire to control everything in our lives that makes us fret and worry about the outcome of any new connection. We burden it with all our expectations and then wonder why it collapses under the strain of our fears and anxieties.

By the way, how do you know that your new soulmate is 'wonderful', you might ask?

You really don't, unless you are together for a while. But by having the expectation of it and focusing upon the positive you will get what you desire because you are in control of those thoughts. If you expect the worst, you will encourage those negative thoughts to become a self-fulfilling prophecy, just as surely as night follows day! Better to think of great things and a lovely person because that is what you are likely to receive, so long as you are not expecting perfection.

※ ※ ※ ※ ※ ※

*Don't fall in love with somebody who doesn't love you back (it's not cool).*

Herbie John

Finding Your Ideal Soulmate!                    241

## Learning to Forgive and to Trust

Most importantly, if you are not wrapped up in the past dwelling on your pain, then you won't expect that every person you meet is out to hurt you. You will accept that everyone is a unique individual who will behave differently. After all, everything we do, no matter how bad, comes out of a good intention. So the goodwill is there from the beginning. You will also allow yourself to get to know that person before judging them negatively. It is our thoughts that attract people to us and thoughts have the power to become self-fulfilling prophecies.

If we have been betrayed by someone in the past, like the man who kept telling everyone how his wife ran off with someone and left him, the only kind of people he is likely to attract are those who show him great sympathy, but also run off and leave him later on, which then confirms his worst expectations! They would have gradually discovered how negative he was, how uncaring and how blaming he had become. He would have been stuck back there, never letting go of the memories until they colour his view of life and rob him of his future.

Talk about the past as much as you like, but always from a position of strength and celebration, not of weakness and victimhood. In this way you allow room for accepting the part you played in your past, as well as the new enriching experiences you still have to come.

Commitment is a mark of confidence. Of knowing who you are, where you are going and how you wish your life to be. By being confident and assured you also give confidence to others, especially the confidence to trust in what is possible.

If you keep putting off commitment to someone you really care about, what exactly are you worried about? What is the worst that could happen to you? What do you really fear about the future? Are you waiting until a perfect time for you to be committed to someone? To perhaps get married? Or to set up home together? How do you know that you will be alive at that time in the future?

The only perfect time for doing something which matters to you is TODAY because it will reveal the results much quicker. More importantly, today could be the last day you have on earth! Additionally, that soulmate will know how you feel and is likely to affirm you in return.

~~~~~~~~~~~~~~~~~~~~~~~~~~~~~~~~~~~

### *Exercise Ten*

So how do you feel about commitment? Would you be comfortable about committing to someone you might meet shortly, without any strings or delays? Find out by going back to Exercise Eight in which you had to rate your fears. What did you give to 'Commitment'?

If it was a four or five, you need to list what you fear most right now relating to your date or partner and try to face each of these fears in turn. Try to reduce their power over you by minimising their size in your head and exploring why they have such effect on you. Make those frightening images of fear as small as possible, turn them into silly items which make you laugh, or replace them with things that make you happy.

If your fears relate to the past, you need to resolve those issues before you carry on with your life, otherwise they will always be dogging your every move. You really would need to leave them behind to have any kind of peaceful life.

244

Remember that no one can go back in time to change events in any way, and that we only get what we focus upon. So you can change your own life by removing your focus from the past to the present day and on to something more positive. It will not only let you feel much better, it will also draw other positive people to you as well.

Always remember that you need to forgive and forget in order to forge ahead.

~~~~~~~~~~~~~~~~~~~~~~~~~~~~~~~~~~

## **REFLECTION**

Step 10 in *Finding Your Ideal Soulmate*....

### *BE COMMITTED!*

.... You will allow love, trust, respect and content-ment to permeate every aspect of your world, thereby truly enjoying the life you have.

✳ ✳ ✳ ✳ ✳ ✳

*Love and magic have a great deal in common.*
*They enrich the soul, delight the heart.*
*And they both take practice.*

Nora Roberts

# ~ POSTSCRIPT ~

## A Letter to David

(*Sent after a year of being apart.*)

My Dear David

**T**onight I read something that challenged me greatly and so I thought I would rise to the challenge. It came from Dr Wayne Dyer's *Real Magic*[11] book and this is what it said:

"What do you have to give away? Keeping in mind that your purpose is always about giving, loving and serving in some capacity, regardless of what vocation you have chosen, this question of what you will be able to give away as your purposeful mission is paramount. It does not take any extra special intelligence to know the simple truth. You cannot give away what you do not have. If you don't have love, harmony and peace within you, then you simply cannot contribute those qualities. So what do you have to give away?"

Fired up by his challenge, I asked myself his question, especially as we are apart, delving deep within my subconscious, past my natural defences, and came up with something even more surprising: 40 things I noticed about you, some of which I wasn't even aware of when we were together and didn't even realise I had noticed. But they were there in my subconscious – 40 things I never realised I loved about you. Forty wonderful things you perhaps don't even know you possessed!

Well, my dear David, I hand them over now freely with all the love I have ever had for you. Enjoy!

### 40 Things I Love
#### .... *about the man who's captured my heart!*

1.  The warm sensual touch of his hands
2.  His tactile, loving nature
3.  The sound of his cheeky little chuckle
4.  His constant encouragement
5.  His genuine care and attention

*10 Easy Steps To....*

6. His never-ending curiosity
7. His amazing listening skills
8. His impressive summarising and paraphrasing skills
9. The way he says 'I love you' and means it
10. The kisses he blows over dinner
11. The way he constantly smiles at me in wonder
12. His rivetingly deep green eyes
13. His beautifully smooth skin
14. His terrific, youthful body
15. His kisses on my neck when I am cooking, relaxing and in bed
16. His gorgeous soft bum
17. The way he gazes at me lovingly
18. Every time he tells me how beautiful I am
19. His unbelievably sexy kisses that reduce me to jelly
20. His ecstatic, delicious shags
21. His wide all-embracing smile
22. The long sweet chats on the phone
23. The long loving hugs in bed
24. The way he says "Yes, My Darling"
25. His warm close embraces
26. His constant communication and discussions
27. His pure unselfishness and generosity

28. His unending vision, creativity and talent

29. The yearning way he looks at me sometimes

30. The way he shares my dreams and aspirations

31. The feel of his sensual body against mine

32. His infectious enthusiasm

33. His impatience and whingeing

34. His confidence and determination

35. His amazing intellect

36. The silences between us that need no words

37, His quirky and unexpected humorous asides

38. The feel of his lovely hair against me

39. The way he turns me on just by thinking
    about him

40. Just being himself, a truly wonderful,
    loving being.

And the last words go to Dr Dyer again: "Just for a short period of time replace doubting and fearing with knowing and trusting. All your doubts are obstacles inhibiting your entry into the kingdom of real magic. Just know and trust and let the doubts others offer solidify your own knowing.

"Look at the life of the doubters and ask yourself if that is what you want as a model for what you can achieve. Then look at the lives of the

*10 Easy Steps To....*

'knowers' and see the difference. The knowers are out there making a difference in their lives – exercising, being healthy and shocking the world with their grand accomplishments. The doubters are generally sitting around behaving in their accustomed role of critic."

Goodnight, dear David, and hope you are having the most joyous week.

Elaine xxx

~~~~~~~~~~~~~~~~~~~~~~~~~~~~~~~~~~~

### **YOUR Challenge Now:**

If you had to think up 40 things about your current spouse, soulmate or date, could you do it this minute? You might not express them in the open way I do, but what would they be, and could you find even more than I did?

If you have found them, what's stopping you from telling him or her and making that person feel special TODAY? It could be the last thing they hear from anyone!

The next thing is to review each step to see where your strengths and weaknesses lie; what is missing or what is in abundance. What could you improve TODAY? List all the things you could easily do to improve that friendship or relationship. Release all those fearful masks you have been wearing and begin to LIVE! It is guaranteed not only to make you feel more empowered and valued, but also to have an impact on your date, your spouse or the even person you fell in love with some time ago and to whom you may have lacked the courage to commit. Try it!

I hope you are now feeling more inspired after reading *10 Easy Steps To....Finding Your Ideal Soulmate!* If you haven't yet done so, I hope you feel able to find that very special someone to share your life, or you are able to make your relationships more fulfilling, enjoyable and greatly motivating. Having taken the trouble to read this through, you certainly deserve your good fortune and happiness. Good Luck!

✳ ✳ ✳ ✳ ✳ ✳

*There are no guarantees.*
*From the viewpoint of fear, none are strong*
*enough. From the viewpoint of love,*
*none are necessary.*

Emmanuel

# References

1. National Statistics (2004) *Social Trends.*

2. Andreas, Steve and Faulkner, Charles(1996) *NLP: The New Technology of Achievement.* Nicholas Brealey Publishing

3. Robbins, Anthony (1989) *Unlimited Power.* Simon & Schuster Ltd.

4. Mintel (2000). *Dating Agencies - UK - February 2000* Leisure Report.

5. Sihera, Elaine (2005) *Money, Sex & Compromise.* AnSer Publishing.

6. Sibson, J.H Gareth (2005) *Single White Failure.* AuthorHouse

7. Andreas, Steve and Faulkner, Charles(1996) *NLP: The New Technology of Achievement.* Nicholas Brealey Publishing

8. Sihera, Elaine (2005) *Money, Sex & Compromise.* AnSer Publishing.

9. Jeffers, Susan, (1991) *Feel the Fear And Do it Anyway.* Rider

10. Allen, James, (2004) *The Wisdom of James Allen: As A Man Thinketh.* Laurel Creek Press

11. Dyer, Wayne Dr (1993). *Real Magic.* First Harper Paperbacks

*10 Easy Steps To....*

# Public Speaking and Seminars
## Elaine is available for the following:

1. *Diversity Consultancy to improve Equality Practice*
2. *Relationship Counselling and Advice*
3. *Empowerment Agent/Career Development Coach*
4. *Leadership Workshops on HR Management*
5. *Media commentator as 'expert' or panelist*

Elaine is also featured in monthly 2 hour sessions of:
**"An Audience with Elaine Sihera"**
presenting the following hot topics:

**A**. *10 Easy Steps To....Understanding Diversity!*
   (Lunchtime Event)

**B**. *10 Easy Steps To....Finding Your Ideal Soulmate!*
   (Anytime)

**C**. *Life certainly begins at 40, 50 or 60....*
   *10 Easy Steps to Enjoying it!* (Lunchtime Event)

**D**. *10 Easy Steps To...Better Confidence & Self Esteem*
   *Your Goals* (Lunchtime Event)

**TO BOOK ELAINE** for your organisation, or to find out the next date of her presentations, please contact:

**Mike Peters, Tiemo Entertainments. Call 07981-577716**
**Email**: info@tiemo.co.uk **OR** elaine@diversityleaders.org.uk

### OR visit: www.elainesihera.com